JOHN FIELD

Discovering
Place-names

SHIRE PUBLICATIONS LTD

Contents

British Library Cataloguing in Publication Data
Field, John, *1921 —*
    Discovering place-names — 3rd ed. —
    (Discovering series; no. 102)
    1. Names, Geographical — Great Britain
    2. English language etymology — Names
    I. Title
    914.1'00142 DA645
    ISBN 0-85263-702-0

Published in 1994 by Shire Publications Ltd, Cromwell House, Church Street, Princes Risborough, Buckinghamshire HP27 9AJ, UK.
Copyright © 1984 by John Field. First edition published 1971. Second edition 1976; reprinted 1978 and 1980. Third edition, revised and expanded, 1984; reprinted 1989; reprinted with changes 1994. Number 102 in the Discovering series. ISBN 0 85263 702 0.
Printed in Great Britain by CIT Printing Services, Press Buildings, Merlins Bridge, Haverfordwest, Dyfed SA61 1XF.

Abbreviations

In the text place-names in England are followed by an abbreviation denoting the county in which the place is situated. Where two county abbreviations separated by an oblique stroke are given, this indicates that the place was transferred to a different county under the local government reorganisation of 1974, or in some cases earlier; the original county is the first named. Where two or more counties separated by commas are given, this indicates that the place-name occurs in each of the counties named.

For place-names in Wales only the new county is given and for those in Scotland only the present administrative region. The old counties for places in Wales and Scotland will, however, be found in the index.

Abbreviations of counties and regions

Abd	Aberdeenshire	Du	Durham
Ang	Anglesey	Dyf	Dyfed
Angus	Angus	ELo	East Lothian
Arg	Argyll	ERY	East Riding, Yorkshire
Av	Avon	Ess	Essex
Ayr	Ayrshire	ESus	East Sussex
Bd	Bedfordshire	Fife	Fife
Bdrs	Borders	Flt	Flintshire
Bk	Buckinghamshire	Gd	Gwynedd
Bnf	Banffshire	Gl	Gloucestershire
Brec	Breconshire	GL	Greater London
Brk	Berkshire	Glam	Glamorgan
Bte	Bute	GM	Greater Manchester
Bwk	Berwickshire	Gra	Grampian
C	Cambridgeshire	Gt	Gwent
Cai	Caithness	H&W	Hereford and Worcester
Card	Cardiganshire	Ha	Hampshire
Carm	Carmarthenshire	He	Herefordshire
Cba	Cumbria	Hld	Highland
Cen	Central	Hrt	Hertfordshire
Ch	Cheshire	Hu	Huntingdonshire
Cla	Clackmannanshire	Hum	Humberside
Clev	Cleveland	Inv	Inverness-shire
Clw	Clwyd	IOM	Isle of Man
Co	Cornwall	K	Kent
Crn	Caernarvonshire	Kcb	Kirkcudbrightshire
Cu	Cumberland	Kcd	Kincardineshire
D&G	Dumfries and Galloway	Knr	Kinross-shire
Db	Derbyshire	L	Lincolnshire
Den	Denbighshire	La	Lancashire
Dev	Devon	Lei	Leicestershire
Dmf	Dumfriesshire	Lnk	Lanarkshire
Dnb	Dunbartonshire	Lo	Lothian
Do	Dorset	Mer	Merseyside

ABBREVIATIONS

MGlam	Mid Glamorgan	So	Somerset
MLo	Midlothian	Sr	Surrey
Mon	Monmouthshire	St	Staffordshire
Mont	Montgomeryshire	Stl	Stirlingshire
Mor	Morayshire	Sut	Sutherland
Mrn	Merioneth	SYk	South Yorkshire
Mx	Middlesex	T&W	Tyne and Wear
Nai	Nairnshire	Tsd	Tayside
Nb	Northumberland	W	Wiltshire
Nf	Norfolk	Wa	Warwickshire
NRY	North Riding, Yorkshire	We	Westmorland
		WGlam	West Glamorgan
Nt	Nottinghamshire	WI	Western Isles
Nth	Northamptonshire	Wig	Wigtownshire
NYk	North Yorkshire	WLo	West Lothian
Ork	Orkney	WM	West Midlands
Oxf	Oxfordshire	Wo	Worcestershire
Peb	Peeblesshire	WRY	West Riding, Yorkshire
Pem	Pembrokeshire		
Per	Perthshire	WSus	West Sussex
Pws	Powys	Wt	Isle of Wight
R	Rutland	WYk	West Yorkshire
Rad	Radnorshire		
Rnf	Renfrewshire		
Ross	Ross and Cromarty	**Other abbreviations**	
Rox	Roxburghshire	ME	Middle English
Sa	Shropshire	OE	Old English
Scl	Strathclyde	OF	Old French
Sf	Suffolk	OIr	Old Irish
SGlam	South Glamorgan	ON	Old Norse
She	Shetland	OW	Old Welsh
Slk	Selkirkshire		

ACKNOWLEDGEMENTS

Sincere thanks are offered to Dr Margaret Gelling and Dr Oliver Padel for advice on particular names and problems. Help was also provided by the following scholars, all of whom are now deceased: Professor John McN. Dodgson (London), Mrs Deirdre Flanagan (Belfast), Mr Eamonn de hÓir (Dublin), Professor Bedwyr Lewis Jones (Bangor), Professor Tomás Ó Máille (Galway) and Professor Melville Richards (Bangor).

4

1. Names and meanings

A natural curiosity about our environment often includes the desire to understand the meaning of names, whether of people or of places. Consulting an ordinary dictionary does not greatly help; the separate parts of **Bloomsbury** (Mx/GL), for instance, or of **Blindcrake** (Cu/Cba) seem to be words that the dictionary would include, but if we define them individually we are no nearer the meaning of the place-name. And what could we do about a name like **Blencogo** (Cu/Cba)? Although an encyclopaedia sometimes provides the meaning of a name, it usually confines itself to historical and geographical information about the place concerned. This book offers brief explanations of a large number of place-names in the British Isles and attempts also to show how the meanings are determined.

To establish the meaning of **Blencogo**, we might argue like this: the parts of this name represent no recognisable English word, and so they may have been modified over (perhaps) a long period of time. If so, we could try to work out what the name had been altered from — and might indeed make some plausible suggestions — but we should be left with the feeling that anyone else's conjecture might be better than ours. Alternatively, we might collect the earliest forms of the name and try to draw conclusions from them. This is how place-name investigators do proceed, tracing occurrences of the name as far back as possible and then inspecting the forms obtained. A knowledge of the early stages of the language or languages involved will enable the roots to be traced from which the name or its parts originated.

There sometimes seems to be an incredible leap to a strange (and even disappointing) conclusion, but the place-name specialist should always be willing to explain the steps in the argument, the changes that have occurred in sound and spelling, the possible reasons for abrupt alterations and why, occasionally, no interpretation is possible. In many place-names it is not clear whether the first element is a reference to a person or is an element closely resembling a personal name.

Blencogo is one of the great number of place-name compounds containing elements from two languages. To an original Celtic name, *Blencog,* 'cuckoo hill', the Norse *haugr*, 'mound', was added by people who did not realise that the hill or burial mound referred to was already so described in the earlier name. The same first element, meaning 'hill, summit', is found in **Blindcrake** (Cu/Cba), 'rocky summit', the second part of the name being Old Welsh *creic*, 'crag, rock', which occurs also in **Creake** (Nf) and **Crick** (Nth).

Many place-names are much easier to deal with than these. The meanings of **Southend** (Ess), **Northwood** (Mx/GL), **High-**

bridge (So), **Newcastle** (Nb/T&W, St) and **Whiteparish** (W) can be found by defining the separate parts of each name. The same applies to **Mudford** (So) and the frequent name **Sandford**, 'muddy ford' and 'sandy ford' respectively. **Saltford** (So/Av) seems to have been so called, however, not from the salinity of the water or the nature of the soil, but because salt was carried across it. These slight differences underline a distinction to be made again and again between the *meaning* of the word (the dictionary definition of the term or its parts) and the *significance* of the name (how it came to be applied, and what conclusions can be drawn from the use of that name for a particular place). Full interpretations require (if possible) the identification and location of features referred to in the names, such as discovering precisely where the fords were which gave Oxford, Guildford and Stratford their names, when and where the original bridge was built at Cambridge or Axbridge or West Bridgford, and what are the reference points of places called Easton, Weston, Norton and Sutton.

Investigation of the early forms of names avoids the pitfalls of 'obvious' meanings. If we learn that *-ham* is a frequent place-name termination, meaning 'village, estate, homestead', it is tempting to treat names like **Oakham** (R/Lei) as self-explanatory; 'oak village' would be an 'obvious' interpretation, but when we discover that it was *Ocham* in 1067 the connection with oak trees can be safely ruled out: 'oak' was still *āc* at that date, and for some time afterwards. **Sevenoaks** (K), for instance, was *Sevenac* in 1200, and as **Oakworth** (WRY/WYk) was *Acurde* in Domesday Book (1086) it can safely be read as 'oak enclosure'; but the early forms of both **Ockham** (Sr) and **Oakham** point to a personal name as first element and tell us that they were the estates or villages of men called Occa or Oca.

The individual syllables of **Bloomsbury** (Mx/GL) seem to be ordinary words, the meanings of which can be obtained from a dictionary. Experience will tell us, however, that *-bury* is often found as a place-name termination, from Old English *burh*, 'fortification' — developing the sense of 'fortified manor house' during the middle ages and later coming to be applied to any manor, whether fortified or not. Early forms of Bloomsbury indicate that it was held by the de Blemund family, from Blémont in France. **Barnsbury, Finsbury** and **Brondesbury** (all Mx/GL), like **Chambersbury** and **Jenningsbury** (Hrt), are similarly manorial tenants' names compounded with *burh*.

A mingling of nationalities and languages has produced a vast and complex collection for study. Names of Celtic, Old English, Scandinavian, Norman-French and Latin origin occur (in various proportions) in all parts of the British Isles. In this book an attempt will be made to explore the contributions made by successive invaders and settlers. The interpretations offered are based on the latest information available. It is a sign of life in these studies that revisions are necessary from time to time, particularly if we look beneath the surface meanings to the historical significance of the names.

2. The counties of England

County boundaries in the United Kingdom underwent great changes between 1964 and 1974. Names introduced at the reorganisation are discussed in chapter 12.

Apart from the 'shires' (of which there are more than twenty) the names of the ancient counties of England can be studied in groups, according to common features in their form and meaning. Of the three northern counties with names ending in *-land*, only one, **Northumberland**, 'territory of the people living north of the Humber', retains its previous designation. The county now known as **Cumbria** includes **Cumberland,** 'land of the *Cymry*', and **Westmorland**, 'territory of the Westmorings' (as well as part of Lancashire). The *Cymry* of north-west England were a Celtic people, akin to those now called the Welsh. The Old English version of their name is the first element in **Cumberland**; it is latinised in the present county name and (with a slight alteration) in *Cambria*, the poetic term for Wales used from the middle ages onwards.

In the counties just mentioned, and in **Devon** and **Cornwall**, the territory is called after the inhabitants, but there is no trace of the 'people' idea in the modern name of Westmorland. There were, however, two additional and highly significant syllables in its tenth-century form, *Westmoringaland*, for the folk-name *Westmoringas* signified 'people of the western moor'. The element *-ing* in many modern names conveys this or a similar meaning, as will be explained in a later chapter.

The names of other counties also commemorate tribes of long ago. **Norfolk** and **Suffolk** mean 'north folk' and 'south folk', referring to the northern and southern peoples of the East Angles; the East, Middle and South Saxons are accounted for in the names of **Essex**, **Middlesex** and **Sussex** respectively. **Wessex**, the name of the old West Saxon kingdom, did not become a county name, though it is now used in the titles of various regional boards and other authorities. Two county names end in *-set*, from Old English *sǣte*, 'settlers, inhabitants': **Somerset** originally meant 'settlers near **Somerton** — the summer dwelling place', and **Dorset** 'settlers near Dorn (Dorchester)'.

Kantion, the ancient name of **Kent** mentioned by Greek

geographers, possibly signifies 'land on the rim or edge'. **Devon** commemorates the *Dumnonii*, known to the Saxons as *Deofnas*, perhaps 'deep ones', alluding to the mining of tin. **Cornwall** will be discussed in the next chapter. **Surrey**, 'southern district' (of Middlesex), contains the term *gē*, 'district', obsolete at an early period but surviving also in **Vange** (Ess), 'fen district', and **Ely** (C), 'eel district'.

The counties whose names end in *-shire* extend in an unbroken block from the Lake District to the English Channel. This area excludes all the counties so far mentioned. **Rutland**, now deprived of its county status, is a lone *-land* name amid the enveloping shires; the ending signifies merely 'estate' rather than 'tract of country, territory', and the first syllable perpetuates the memory of Rota, an early lord.

Shire (Old English *scîr),* meaning '(administrative) division', is also an element in the names of many former counties in Wales and Scotland and sometimes occurs in the designations of smaller areas in England, usually ancient feudal territories, such as **Richmondshire** and **Hallamshire**. The first part of *-shire* county names is normally that of the chief town, so that **Oxfordshire**, for instance, may be interpreted as 'administrative region centred upon Oxford'. Usually the county-town name appears in its normal form, as in **Leicestershire**, **Worcestershire** and **Derbyshire**; but sometimes there is a slight adjustment. **Wiltshire** was *Wiltescire* in Domesday Book, but documents of the ninth and tenth centuries refer to *Wiltunscir*, showing the dependence of the region on **Wilton**, 'estate on the river Wylye'; in **Lancashire** and **Cheshire**, **Lancaster** and **Chester** are similarly modified.

The connection between **Shropshire** and its county town is clearer when we find that the early form of **Shrewsbury** was *Scrobbesbyrig*, 'fortified place in scrubland', and the county was called *Scrobbesbyrigscir* in the eleventh century. The Normans found both names difficult to pronounce and so they turned them into *Salopesberia* and *Salopescira*, the latter giving rise to the contracted form **Salop**, for a time the official name of the reorganised county. In **Hampshire** also it is hard to discern the name of the county town. **Southampton** was formerly *Hamtun*, but by the eleventh century it became necessary to distinguish it from another *Hamtun* (**Northampton**) by the respective prefixes *South* and *North*; by 1086 the southern county had become *Hantescir* (whence the contracted form **Hants**), but the midland one generally used the full form. The distinction might not have been needed if Southampton had remained *Homwic*, as it was called in ancient annals. **Berkshire**, the only *-shire* name not derived from that of the county town, recalls the upland forest known as *Barroc*, from a Celtic word meaning 'hilly'.

Names of county towns are of various origins. **Derby** is Scandinavian, but there was earlier an English name, *North-worthy*; the Danish settlers evidently thought 'deer farm' more suitable for their military centre than 'north enclosure'. The origin of **York** is much more ancient; the Celtic name, *Eburacum*, possibly meaning 'yew grove', was adapted by Anglian settlers to *Eoforwic*, an intelligible Old English term meaning 'boar farm'; in due course Scandinavians further modified the English name to *Jórvik*. By the thirteenth century the last form had become *Yeork* and soon developed into the name as we now have it. This Celtic name is outstanding in the way its formation concisely records the history of early England. The name **Durham** is unique in England in being shared by county and town. Originally *Dunholm*, an Anglo-Scandinavian hybrid meaning 'hill island', the name was modified to something like its present form by the Normans. Their *Durelme* or *Dureaume* was given a more English appearance by the *-ham* spelling adopted in recent centuries. **Carlisle** (Cu), **Exeter** (Dev), and **Bodmin** (Co) have Celtic roots. Like Derby, **Appleby**, 'farmstead by an apple tree', the chief town of the former county of Westmorland, bears a Scandinavian name. Names with an Old English origin include **Taunton** (So), 'farm on the river Tone', **Lewes** (Sx), 'the tumuli', and **Maidstone** (K), 'the stone of the maidens'. The names of other county towns will be discussed in later chapters.

The **Isle of Wight** bears an ancient name of uncertain significance. The British root-word means 'turn, course', perhaps referring to the position of the island in the fork of the Solent. The **Isles of Scilly** were also alluded to by ancient writers, but some references are as uncertain as the meaning of the name. The spelling with *Sc-* is recent and does not clarify the history of the word.

The largest shires were each subdivided into three sections, which later became administrative counties. The Yorkshire **Ridings**, **East**, **West** and **North**, were the 'third parts' of the shire; the Scandinavian *thrithjung*, from which their names are derived, is used in this sense in Norway and Iceland. In time the initial *Th-* attached itself to the preceding word, so that *North Thrithjung* became **North Riding**, and so on. The similar division of Lincolnshire was into the **Parts of Lindsey**, the **Parts of Holland** and the **Parts of Kesteven**. **Lindsey** means '*Lindon* island', *Lindon* being the old name for Lincoln. Lindsey was formerly further divided, like Yorkshire, into Ridings. In **Kesteven** the first part is a British word signifying 'wooded area'; the second is a Scandinavian expression meaning 'meeting place'. **Holland**, 'land by a hill spur', is of English origin.

3. Britons and Romans

When the Romans arrived in Britain they found numerous tribes, usually independent but sometimes bound in loose alliances, and frequently at war among themselves. Most of these people were Celtic, though there was probably also the remnant of an earlier population. Even the Celts were not homogeneous, having come in successive waves from various parts of continental Europe, and their diversity showed itself in differences of language. Some were speakers of Brythonic (or Brittonic) dialects, from which modern Welsh and Breton are derived; others used Goidelic forms of Celtic, represented today by the Gaelic of Ireland, Scotland and the Isle of Man.

Most of the earliest records of British place-names date from the centuries of the Roman occupation. The documents were either in Greek or in Latin, and the exact forms of the names often remain uncertain, owing to the addition of classical terminations to the Celtic word stems.

Although it might be expected that in England fewer names of Celtic origin would survive than in Wales or in Scotland, their numbers are quite large. In addition there are many river-names (to be discussed in a later chapter). The names borne by some counties are wholly or partly Celtic, and those of a substantial number of important towns declare their descent from early British settlements. The meaning of the name of **London**, *Londinium* in the Latin records, is as obscure as the origins of the settlement, which may well have been pre-Celtic. **Dover** (K) was mentioned (as *Dubris*) as early as AD 4. The British word, meaning 'waters', i.e. 'the stream', alludes to the river Dour and not to the English Channel. **Wendover** (Bk), 'white waters', also contains this element and describes the clear chalk stream there. **Andover** (Ha) means '(place on) the stream called *Ann*'; the river is now known as the Anton, because of an eighteenth-century antiquarian's misunderstanding of a Latin text. The early name meant 'ash-tree stream'.

Reculver (K), 'great headland', **Penkridge** (St), 'chief mound', and **Lympne** (K), 'elm place', are a few names surviving in a recognisable form from the earliest period. The usual interpretation of **Catterick** (NRY/NYk) as 'rapids' appears to be confirmed by its nearness to a turbulent part of the river Swale, but the early form *Cataractonium* may be the Latin adaptation of a Celtic name, perhaps meaning 'battle ramparts', rather than the expected 'cataract'. **Eccles** (La/GM), 'church', and a number of compound names with Old English terminations, such as **Eccleston** (Ch, La, La/Mer) and **Ecclesfield** (WRY/SYk) are evidence of the survival of British churches among the pagan

Anglo-Saxons, who borrowed the term *ecles* from their Celtic neighbours.

Lincoln was originally *Lindon*, to which *Colonia* was added during the Roman occupation. The modern name combines the two elements, the first of which means 'pool' and refers to Brayford Pool in the Witham. The Latin addition indicated that this was a place where military veterans could settle. **Carlisle** (Cu/Cba) also contains an early name to which another word has been prefixed. To *Luguvalium*, meaning 'place of Luguvalos', Welsh *caer*, 'fort', was prefixed in the eleventh century. **Leeds** (WRY/WYk) differs only slightly from its Celtic original, *Loidis*, 'district of the river'. The early name was applied to the region around the modern city, the location of the British kingdom of **Elmet**. This name occurs as an affix in **Sherburn in Elmet** (WRY/NYk) and **Barwick in Elmet** (WRY/WYk) but its origin and meaning are obscure.

Many place-names of British origin consist of a Celtic stem to which has been added an English (or other) suffix. There is the large class of names ending in *-chester* (or *-caster*, *-cester*, etc). Although the majority of names with this termination refer to former Roman towns or military stations, the ending is not directly derived from the Latin word *castra*, 'camp', as is sometimes thought, nor was that term used in Britain by the Romans for naming purposes, except for one place in Cumberland (*Castra Exploratorum*, 'camp or fort of the scouts'). Old English *ceaster* was adapted from the Latin word by the Anglo-Saxons while they were still on the continent and was used by them in their new homeland to designate former Roman towns. Not every modern name ending in *-chester* belongs to this class. **Grantchester** (C) has a completely different origin, as will be explained in a later chapter.

A few places bear a contracted British name followed by *-ceaster*. They include **Gloucester** (*Glevum*, 'bright place'), **Brancaster** (Nf) (*Branodunum*, 'fort of the crow'), **Manchester** (La/GM) (*Mamucio*, 'breast-shaped hill'), **Doncaster** (WRY/SYk) (*Danum*, 'fast-flowing river') and **Dorchester** (Do) (*Durnovaria*, perhaps 'pebbly place'). In **Lanchester** (Du) (*Longovicium*, 'place of the *Longovices*, "shipfighters" ') the first element is the name of the tribe, as also in **Worcester** (*Wigora*) and **Leicester** (*Ligora*). The obscure element *venta* occurs in the British names for **Winchester** (Ha, *Venta Belgarum*), **Caister St Edmunds** (Nf, *Venta Icenorum*) and **Caerwent** (Mon/Gt, *Venta Silurum*). Only in **Winchester** (Ha) is the *-chester* termination combined with this element but **Caister** (Nf), like **Caistor** in Lincolnshire, is derived from *ceaster*, and in **Caerwent** (Mon/Gt) the related Welsh word has been prefixed. *Venta* is often interpreted 'market', but the meaning is uncertain; the examples imply that the term was used of tribal centres — for the Belgae at Winchester, the Iceni at Caister, and the Silures at Caerwent.

Wroxeter (Sa) (*Viroconium*) may have a Celtic personal name as its first element; Anglo-Saxon lords named Godmund, Cēna and Wittuc are commemorated in **Godmanchester** (Hu/C), **Kenchester** (He/H&W) and **Uttoxeter** (St). The names of local rivers combine with *ceaster* in **Lancaster** (La) (**Lune**, 'health-giving'), **Exeter** (Dev) (**Exe**, 'water'), **Towcester** (Nth) (**Tove**, 'dilatory one') and **Frocester** (Gl) (**Frome**, 'fair river'). **Chester** (Ch) was *Deva* in the ancient records, 'place on the Dee', but received an early Welsh name, *Cair Legion*, from its having been the headquarters of the Twentieth Legion. The Old English *Legacæstir* was a translation of this but was confused with *Ligoraceaster* (Leicester). The distinguishing element in the name of Chester was therefore omitted.

In **Salisbury** (W) and **Lichfield** (St) an English suffix is added to a Celtic root. The meaning of the first element of *Sorbiodunum* is not known, but *dunum*, meaning 'fort', was rendered by the Anglo-Saxons as *burh*; the Old English version of the entire name, *Searobyrg*, was transformed into *Salesbiri* by the Normans. In *Liccidfeld*, the eighth-century form of **Lichfield**, the Old English word *feld*, 'open country', is added to a British name, *Letocetum*, 'grey wood'; **Lytchett** (Do) and **Litchett** (Ha), 'grey wood', contain the same Celtic root.

Cornwall consists of *Cornovii*, a Celtic tribal name possibly meaning 'promontory folk', to which Old English *wealas*, '(Celtic-speaking) foreigners', was added. Many names in the county, including those of the larger towns, are of Celtic origin. **Bude** is derived from a British river-name of unknown meaning. **Bodmin**, 'dwelling of the sanctuary', alludes to the local monastery, said to have been founded by King Athelstan in 926. **Penzance**, 'holy headland', is so called on account of the central position of its church on the shore. **Mevagissey** is '(church of) St Mew and St Ida', celebrating, like other names on the peninsula, saints who flourished there in the early middle ages. Several parishes are dedicated to St Peran: **Perranporth** is 'St Peran's port', **Perranarworthal** is 'St Peran in the marsh' and **Perranzabuloe** is 'St Peran in the sand', the affix here being the Latin *in sabulo*.

Other Cornish names relating to geographical features include **Camborne**, 'crooked hill', **Looe**, 'inlet of the sea', and **Redruth**, 'red ford'. **Fowey** is 'beech river', **Penryn**, 'promontory' and **Pentire (Point)**, 'the end of the land'. Cornish *pen* is 'head, top, summit', also 'point, promontory', but the meaning of the second element in **Penwith**, the old name for **Land's End**, is unknown.

Marazion is 'little market'; the name of its former neighbour

Market Jew (*Marchadyou*, 1200, from Cornish *marchas, dyow*) survives in a street name in Penzance and means 'southern market'. **Liskeard**, 'court of Carud', is similar in appearance to **Liscard** (Ch/Mer); the second element of the latter, however, is Old Welsh *carrec*, 'rock'. The Celtic term for 'court, chief residence' is found also in **Liss** (Ha) and **Lizard** (Co), 'high court' or 'high stronghold'. **Lesnewth** (Co) is 'new hall'.

Names beginning with *Tre-*, 'farm, village', are frequent in Cornwall but are not peculiar to the county, and derivatives of Welsh *tref, tre*, related to Cornish *trev*, are to be found in other parts of Britain. **Treales** (La), like **Treflys** in Gwynedd, means 'homestead of the court'. **Tremaine** (Co), 'farm of the stone', has counterparts in Dyfed (**Tremain**) and Cumbria (**Triermain**, formerly in Cumberland). The common Old English *tūn* has been affixed to these components in **Trematon**. The second element in **Tregony** is obscure, and that in **Tregavethan** may be a Cornish personal name. Occasionally Old English personal names were added, as in **Trehawke, Trehunsey** and **Trekinnard**, containing respectively Heafoc, Hunsige and Cyneheard.

In **Treneglos**, 'village with the church', the *-n-* is from the Cornish definite article *an*. Early spellings of **Terregles** (Kcb/ D&G), which has the same meaning (e.g. *Travereglys*, 1365), also retain an article (though here it is Welsh *yr*), as do those of **Tranent** (ELo/Lo), 'village of the streams' (e.g. *Trauernent*, 1127). **Trenowth** (Co) is 'new farm', but in 'old farm', **Hendra**, *trev* is placed after its qualifier. **Truro** does not belong to this group of names; its second element is obscure, and the first is not *trev* but Cornish *tri*, 'three'. The corresponding Welsh word, *tri*, occurs in **Trelleck** (Mon/Gt), 'three stones' — another name whose modern form is misleading. But **Trellick** (Dev) (*Trevelak*, 1249) is derived from *tre*, the second element being possibly the personal name Maeloc, found also in **Trevellick** (Co).

4. Germanic invaders

In the fifth century AD, after numerous raiding expeditions over a long period of time, invaders from northern Germany began to colonise Britain. The arrival of the Anglo-Saxons is sometimes compared to a modern military invasion, but it was probably more like a slowed-down version of the development of North America. The immigrants spread westwards and either established completely new dwelling places or took over existing British villages. More invaders came, and as the population grew more and more land had to be prepared for cultivation, often by the clearance of extensive forests. The progress of this settlement is recorded, at least in part, in the place-names of Britain.

The tribal names borne by the newcomers are embodied in such county names as **Essex** and **Sussex**, already discussed. The Angles, who occupied the Midlands and the North, provided a name for the entire country: **England** is 'land of the Angles'. From Old English *East Engle*, 'eastern Angles', **East Anglia** is the regular, though unofficial, term for an area now including Norfolk, Suffolk, Cambridgeshire and (illogically) Essex. It is even more illogical to use the designation **Anglia** for this area (as several commercial users do), since this, the Latin name for England, refers to the entire country, not to a portion of it.

Colonies of Angles among Saxons or Cumbrian Britons were given such names as **Englefield** (Brk), **Englebourne** (Dev) and **Inglewood (Forest)** (Cu/Cba) — respectively 'open country', 'stream' and 'wood' of the Angles. Settlements of Saxons in alien territory received names like **Saxton** (C, WRY/NYk), 'estate of the Saxon(s)', **Saxham** (Sf), 'village of the Saxons', **Saxondale** (Nt), 'valley of the Saxons', and possibly **Seisdon** (St), 'hill of the Saxons'. **Exton** (Ha) was originally a settlement of East Saxons in Wessex and was recorded in 940 as *East Seaxnatune*; in Domesday Book **Exton** (R/Lei), however, was *Exentune*, probably meaning 'oxen farm'.

Advances in name studies and archaeology have led to a radical revision of the chronology of place-names in England. Much research has concentrated on comparing the distribution of names of various types with the location of pagan Anglo-Saxon cemeteries, major rivers (important routes for invaders by sea) and Roman roads. It is no longer thought that the oldest place-names are those whose early forms consisted of a personal name followed by *-ingas*, 'followers of ———', as in **Yalding** (K), **Hastings** (ESus), **Reading** (Brk) or **Poynings** (WSus), 'followers of' (respectively) Ealda, Hæsta, Rēada, or Pūna. Other examples are **Havering** (Ess/GL), **Barking** (Ess/GL, Sf), **Braughing** (Hrt), **Elsing** (Nf) and **Cooling** (K). The identities of these leaders are irretrievably lost, though some individuals lending their names in later place nomenclature are on independent record. Such names belong to an early stage of the settlement, but not to the first period of colonisation. The groups were probably small, perhaps no more than extended families, as *-ingas* names are numerous in certain places. Within a restricted area in West Sussex, **Worthing**, **Lancing**, **Angmering** and **Goring** refer to territory occupied by the followers, dependants or families of Worth, Wlanc, Angenmǣr and Gāra.

Places of worship used by the earliest Anglo-Saxon settlers are alluded to in **Harrow** (Mx/GL), **Peper Harow** (Sr) and **Arrow-field** (Wo/H&W), all derived from *hearg*, 'pagan shrine, temple'; from *wēoh* or *wīg*, of the same meaning, are derived **Weedon** (Nth), **Winwood** (Hrt) and **Wye** (K).

Among the categories of names investigated in great detail have been those ending in *-ham*. Most modern names with this termination may be derived from one of two sources: Old English *hām* ('village') and Old English *hamm* ('land in a river bend, water-meadow'). It is impossible to tell one set from the other from modern spellings alone. **Evesham** (Wo/H&W) and **Chippenham** (W), both lying in river bends, are from *hamm*, combined respectively with the personal names Eof and Cippa. **Ham** in its simple form, frequently found in southern England, is also of this origin, together with **East Ham** and **West Ham** (Ess/GL) and **South Hams** (Dev) — all riverside sites. Other names containing this element are **Farnham** (Sr), 'fern-covered water-meadow', on the river Wey, **Topsham** (Dev), 'Toppa's water-meadow', beside the Exe, and **Burnham** (So), 'water-meadow by the stream', on the river **Brue**, 'brisk river'. But **Burnham** (Bk), 'village by a stream', is derived from *hām* and so are **Amersham** (Bk), **Faversham** (K) and **Shoreham** (K), respectively 'Ealhmund's village', 'village of the smith' and 'village by a rock or steep slope'; **(Old) Shoreham** (WSus) is identical in meaning with the last, and so the distinguishing addition in **Shoreham-by-Sea** (WSus) is not redundant.

Early forms indicate the following also to be *hām* derivatives: **Aldenham** (Hrt), **Newnham** (Gl), **Northam** (Dev), **Southam** (Gl), **Eastham** (Ch/Mer) and **Westerham** (K), respectively 'old', 'new', 'north', 'south', 'east' and 'more westerly village'. Many instances of the frequent **Farnham** belong here (but not the one in Surrey, already mentioned). The soil is alluded to in **Flintham** (Nt) and **Stoneham** (Ha); **Greatham** (Du/Clev, Ha) and **Greetham** (L, R/Lei) mean 'village on gravel'. **Garboldisham** (Nf), **Saxmundham** (Sf), **Offham** (K), **Pagham** (WSus), **Fakenham** (Nf), **Dagenham** (Ess/GL) and **Meopham** (K) all contain personal names; **Babraham** (C) has as its first element the woman's name Beaduburg.

Names ending in *-ingham* have their own special problems. First, *hām* names must be distinguished from those ending in *hamm*. The names of two county towns illustrate this distinction: **Nottingham**, 'village of Snot's people', is a *-hām* name. (It has lost its initial *S-* owing to Norman influence.) **Buckingham**, however, from *-hamm*, means 'land in a river bend occupied by Bucca's people'. The town is certainly so situated, as is **Birlingham** (Wo/H&W), '*hamm* belonging to Byrla's people', which lies within a great loop of the Avon; the early spellings *Buccingahamme, Byrlingahamme* confirm this derivation.

Birmingham (Wa/WM), **Billingham** (Du/Clev), **Atcham (Attingham)** (Sa), **Ovingham** (Nb) and **Altrincham** (Ch/GM), 'village of the people of ...' (respectively Beorma, Bill, Eata and Aldhere), are now placed in a single group. They are often identifiable by the local pronunciation, with '-cham' or '-jam' in the final syllable (as in 'Brummagem', frequently heard for **Birmingham** in the West Midlands); the spelling of some of these names suggests this, even though current speech may not (e.g. the pronunciation of **Altrincham** with '-ing-' in the middle). The distinction in early forms between these and the other *-ingham* names is clear, but much work on them remains to be done. **Everingham** (ERY/Hum) and **Gillingham** (K), 'village of the followers of' Eofor or Gylla, join **Nottingham** in the second class of *-ingham* names, with **Empingham** (R/Lei), 'village of the followers of Empa', **Framlingham** (Sf), '... of Framela', **Walsingham** (Nf), '... of Wals', and **Cottingham** (ERY/Hum, Nth), '. . . of Cotta'. Names of this type, though now regarded as older than the *-ingas* group (e.g. Reading), are not considered to be of such antiquity as the *-hām* names, e.g. **Egham** (Sr), 'Ecga's village', **Streatham** (Sr/GL), 'village on the Roman road', or **Grafham** (Hu/C), 'village by a grove'.

A development from *hām* was *hām-tūn*, meaning 'home farm'; the compounds are often self-explanatory, e.g. **Littlehampton** (WSus), **Netherhampton** (W) and **Northampton** (Nth). To these can be added **Meysey Hampton** (Gl) and **Hampton Gay** (Oxf), with manorial affixes, and **Oakhampton** (Wo/H&W). The similar **Okehampton** (Dev), however, is not related to the last example, but was earlier *Ocmundtun*, 'village on the river Okement'. Note that **Southampton** (Ha) is not among these names. The spelling of its early forms *Homtun*, *Homwic* confirms that this is a compound of *hamm*, 'land in a river-bend, meadow', or possibly here, as in some other coastal names, 'promontory'. **Hampton** (Mx/GL), another **Hampton** in Herefordshire (now H&W), as well as **Hampton Bishop** and **Hampton Wafer** in the same county, and **Hampton Lucy** (Wa) were all originally *Hamm-tun*, 'village in or by riverside meadow-land'.

The compound form *hām-stede* is regarded as a unit in many names, e.g. **Hampstead** (Mx/GL, Brk), with its variants **Hamstead** (St/WM, Wt) and **Hempstead** (Ess, Nf). Usually rendered 'homestead, farm', this element is frequently prefixed by the name of a tree or other plant, as in **Ashampstead** (Brk), **Nettlestead** (K), **Nuthampstead** and **Wheathampstead** (Hrt), none of which requires further explanation. Other first elements occurred in **Berkhamsted** (Hrt), probably 'homestead on a hill', and **Easthampstead** (Brk), which is shown by its early forms (e.g.) *Yethamstede* 1176) to be the 'homestead by a gate', namely that to Windsor Forest. **Hemel Hempstead** (Hrt) is 'homestead in Hamel, i.e. broken country'; the district-name, Hamel, was incorporated in some early forms and *Hemlampsted* became *Hempstead*; subsequently *Hemel* was reintroduced as a separate word.

Places bearing *ford* names include many of historical importance. With **Stamford** (L, Nb), 'stone or stony ford', **Stamford Bridge** (YE/Hum) must also be mentioned. **Stamford Bridge** (Mx/GL), however, was originally *Sandford*. **Stratford** (*freq*) means 'ford crossed by a Roman road'. **Strefford** (Sa), **Stretford** (He/H&W, La) and **Trafford** (La/GM) are of the same origin. The two instances of **Burford** (Oxf, Sa), 'ford by a fort', have sometimes been distinguished by the addition of *on the Wold* and *on the Teme* respectively. The first element in **Watford** (Hrt, Nth) signifies 'hunting' and that in **Wallingford** (Brk/Oxf), 'people of Wealh'. **Stafford** means 'ford by a landing place', **Oxford**, 'ford for oxen', **Bedford**, 'Bēda's ford', **Hertford**, 'stag ford', and **Hereford**, 'army ford'. **Guildford** (Sr), 'ford at the golden place', alludes to the colour of the sandy bed at St Catherine's, where the river is crossed by the Pilgrim's Way.

In early days bridges would be built only at much used river crossings, such as those by major towns, and so it is not surprising that there is one county town with a *-bridge* name: **Cambridge** has developed interestingly from Old English *Grantebrycg*, though earlier it was *Grantacaestir*, which invited comparison with **Grantchester** (C). The latter is not a *ceaster* name at all, though clearly **Cambridge** once was! The old name meant 'bridge over the (river) Granta'. Real or imagined difficulties of pronouncing a name containing two consonant clusters (*Gr-* and *-ntbr-*) brought about the present form, and the river name became **Cam** by the process of 'back-formation'. **Grantchester** ('settlers on the Granta') preserves the former river name, to which has been added *sǣte*, 'settlers'.

Another important place with a name alluding to its bridge is **Bristol** (Gl and So/Av). The meaning 'meeting place by the bridge' is not clear from the modern form of the name, the case history of which, from *Brycg stowe* of the eleventh century, through *Bricstou* (1169) to its present spelling, is a classic of name studies. The element *stow* is usually rendered 'place', but it was often applied to sacred sites or assembly places. Spelling and pronunciation interaction produced variants such as *-stou*, *-stoll* and *-stol* for the ending. References to a bridge here occur in twelfth-century documents, but the name itself testifies to the existence of such a structure on the site long before.

Huntingdon, possibly 'huntsman's hill', is no longer a county town, as its shire is now part of Cambridgeshire. The small county enjoyed centuries of independence followed by a few years of union with the **Soke of Peterborough**, also at that time an administrative county. **Peterborough** (Nth/C) means '(Saint) Peter's chartered town', from the dedication of the abbey at *Medeshamstede*, 'Mēda's homestead'. The town became *Burg* when the monastery was rebuilt after destruction by Vikings; the modern name was recorded first in the fourteenth century. The wealthy abbey acquired much of the surrounding territory and its special jurisdiction (OE *socn*) became known as the **Soke of Peterborough**.

The common element *wîc*, 'dwelling, farm, dairy-farm, industrial building', is the second component of **Warwick**, 'dwellings near a weir'. This element also occurs as *-wich*, found in the names of two East Anglian county towns, **Ipswich** (Sf), 'Gip's port', and **Norwich** (Nf), 'northern port' — relative to both Ipswich and Dunwich. This sense of Old English *wîc* occurs also in *Homwic* (an early name for **Southampton**), in **Greenwich** and **Woolwich** (both K/GL) and in **Sandwich** (K). The first elements in the last three names point to natural characteristics ('green' and 'sandy') or to the cargoes being carried ('wool'). In **Dunwich** (Sf), an original form *Domnoc* ('deep place') was adapted by popular etymology to the *Duneuuic* spelling found in Domesday Book; the termination *-wîc* probably made better sense to those who used it, as in the early middle ages Dunwich was a prosperous seaport.

Sometimes *wich* or *wick* has the sense 'outlying (dairy) farm' or even 'industrial place or premises', notably in names relating to salt works in Cheshire and other counties. Direction and location are indicated in **Northwich** (Ch), **Southwick** (Du/T&W, Gl, WSus), and **Westwick** (WRY/NYk), **Middlewich** (Ch) and **Netherwich** (Wo/H&W). Cheesemaking is alluded to in **Cheswick** (Nb), **Chiswick** (Ess, Mx/GL) and **Keswick** (Cu/Cba, Nf, WRY, WYk). **Butterwick** is found in Lincolnshire and Westmorland (now Cumbria). At **Colwich** (St) and **Colwick** (Nt) charcoal was produced. The first element in **Droitwich** (Wo/H&W) means 'dirty', in **Nantwich** (Ch) 'well known', in **Prestwich** (La/GM) and **Prestwick** (Bk, Nb, Ayr/Scl) 'priest', and in **Smethwick** (Ch, St/WM) 'smith'. **Rushwick** (Wo/H&W), **Bromwich** (St/WM, Wa/WM; 'broom'), **Ashwick** (So), **Hazelwick** (WSus), **Appletreewick** (WRY/NYk), **Redwick** (GL/Av, 'reed'), **Benwick** (C, 'beans') and **Slaughterwicks** (Sr - from *slāh-trēow*, 'sloe-tree') are a small selection of the names describing places in terms of trees and other plants.

5. The Anglo-Saxon landscape

Immigrants establishing settlements in the uncultivated countryside might well name their new homes from aspects of the landscape, such as woods, springs and streams. Desirable sites in otherwise uninviting country would also be worthy of mention, and many place-names refer to features such as dry ground amid marshes.

Availability of timber for fuel and shelter would doubtless be considered in choosing a site for settlement, and a good location might be either beside a wood or within a forest clearing. The termination -ley in modern names is often from Old English lēah, 'wood, grove, clearing'. The element, which later developed the sense 'pasture', occurs alone in **Lea** (L), **Lee** (Bk, Ess, Ha, K, Sa) and **Leigh** (frequent); **Leam** (Nb) means 'among the woods'. The plural is found in **Leece** (La/Cba) and **Lees** (La/GM). The common **Bradley** is 'broad wood or grove'; **Henley** (Oxf), **Langley** (frequent) and **Rowley** (Dev, ERY/Hum, St, WRY/WYk) are woods or clearings which are 'high', 'long' and 'rough' respectively.

The oak is named in **Acklam** (ERY/NYk, NRY/Clev), **Acle** (Nf), **Eagle** (L), **Oakleigh** (K), **Oakley** (Bd, Bk, Wo/H&W) and **Ocle** (He/H&W); the birch in **Berkeley** (Gl) and **Berkley** (So). **Ashley** (frequent), **Boxley** (K), **Elmley** (Wo/H&W) and **Thornley** (Du) are self-explanatory. **Lindley** (WRY/WYk) refers to the lime, **Uley** (Gl) to the yew, and **Weedley** (ERY/Hum), **Withiel** (So) and **Willey** (Ch, He/H&W, Sa, Wa) all allude to the willow. But **Willey** (Sr) is a 'glade with a pagan shrine'; **Thursley** (Sr) and **Thundersley** (Ess) were sacred to the god Thunor or Thor. Animal names occur in **Foxley** (He/H&W), **Hartley** (frequent), **Oxley** (St/WM), **Cowley** (Dev, Gl, Oxf), **Horsley** (Db) and **Lambley** (Nt); the badger and the wolf are referred to in **Brockley** (So/Av) and **Woolley** (Brk, Hu/C, WRY/WYk).

Brooks or streams might give their names to settlements in several ways. Occasionally the existing stream name was used for the habitation. **Kennett** (C) and **East** and **West Kennet** (W) are on streams of the same Celtic name, possibly meaning 'exalted one'. **Colne** (La) is from the British river-name, meaning 'roaring stream'. Other sites by rivers are denoted by terminations such as -burn (bourne) or -brook, as in **Ashbourne** (Db), **Blackburn** (La), **Woburn** (Bd), 'crooked stream', **Claybrooke** (Lei), **Sedgebrook** (L) and **With(e)ybrook** (Co, Wa), 'willow stream'.

The frequent -well names refer to springs. They may be cold, as in **Caldwell** (NRY, NYk) or **Chadwell** (Ess); of various colours, such as **Radwell** (Bd, Hrt), **Greenwell** (Dev) or **Whitwell** (Db, Hrt, R/Lei); or they may be visited by wild creatures, as in **Hartwell** (Bk, Dev, Nth), **Frogwell** (Dev), **Goswell** (Mx/GL), **Wrenwell** (Dev) or **Tathwell** (L — 'toad spring').

Fortification was important in the days when territory and survival were almost synonymous, and therefore many place-names refer to strongholds. The Old English word burh was applied to prehistoric earthworks, to former Roman camps and stations, and to defensive works constructed by the Anglo-Saxons themselves. Modern names containing this element include **Bury** (La/GM), the frequent **Brough** and **Burgh** (with various affixes) and many examples terminating in -*b(o)rough*, -*burgh* and -*bury*. Prehistoric camps have been found near some of the many places called **Oldbury** and are alluded to in **Cadbury** (Dev, So), **Cholesbury** (Bk), **Badbury** (Do) and **Banbury** (Oxf), all of which have personal names as first elements. **Canterbury** (K), 'strong-hold of the men of Kent', replaced the British name *Durovernum*, 'walled town by an alder swamp'. Compass points and plant names are found in **Southburgh** (Nf), **Sudbury** (Sf), **Norbury** (frequent), **Westborough** (L), **Westbury** (Bk, Gl, W), **Eastbury** (Brk), **Astbury** (Ch), **Flexbury** (Co), **Thornbury** (He/H&W), **Thornbrough** (Nb) and **Thornborough** (WRY/ NYk). **Woodborough** (Nt) and **Shawbury** (Sa) refer to nearby woods. There are references to Roman stations in **Brough** (Db, Nt, ERY/Hum, NRY/NYk, We/Cba) and **Richborough** (K) — the first syllable of the last being the old name *Rutupiae*, perhaps 'muddy waters'. **Hertingfordbury** (Hrt), alluding to an Anglo-Saxon fortification, was originally *Hertfordingburi*, 'stronghold of the men of Hertford'. Later *burh* came to mean 'fortified (manor)house', 'manor' and then 'town', as in **Prestbury** (Ch) and **Bassettsbury** (Bk). In **Newbury** (Brk) the term has the sense 'chartered borough', as also in **Bury St Edmunds** (Sf), a renaming of *Baedricesworth*, to which the relics of the martyred king were taken.

As a first element *burh* occurs in the frequent **Burton**, 'village by a fortified place or a borough', to which the name of a feudal lord is often added, as in **Burton Fleming** (ERY/Hum) or **Burton Hastings** (Wa). The variant **Bourton** tends to take descriptive rather than feudal, additions; **Bourton on the Water** (Gl), on the Windrush, is near an ancient earthwork.

Some names ending in -*borough* (etc) originate in Old English *beorg*, 'hill, mound'. **Farnborough** (Brk, Ha, K/GL) is 'fern-covered hill'; **Whatborough** (Lei) is 'wheat hill'; **Wadborough** (Wo/H&W) means 'hill on which woad grew'. **Hillborough** (K) seems repetitive, but the first element was once *halig*, 'holy'. **Woodnesborough** (K) was a mound sacred to the god Woden; **Shuckburgh** (Wa), like **Shugborough** (St), means 'hill haunted by goblins'. The hill at **Modbury** (Dev) was used for the *mōt* or assembly, cf. **Modbury Hundred** (Do).

Settlements needed secure boundaries and many names refer to enclosures. One element with this meaning is *worth*, the simple form of which is found in **Worth** (Ch, Do, K, WSus). **Highworth** (W), **Littleworth** (Brk/Oxf) and **Longworth** (Brk/ Oxf) are self-explanatory, as are **Clayworth** (Nt), **Thistleworth** (WSus) and **Duckworth** (La). **Hinxworth** (Hrt) means 'horse enclosure'; **Lindsworth** (Wo/WM) alludes to lime trees and **Turnworth** (Do) to thorn trees. **Minsterworth** (Gl) was a possession of St Peter's monastery in Gloucester. The ending is disguised in **Abinger** (Sr — *Abingewurd*, 1191 — 'enclosure of Eabba's people'), **Chelwood** (So/Av — 'Cēola's enclosure') and **Cotchford** (ESus — 'thicket enclosure'). The most common type of *-worth* name, however, has an Old English personal name as the first element. Examples are **Isleworth** (Mx/GL — Gislere), **Wandsworth** (Sr/GL — Wendel), **Rickmansworth** (Hrt) and **Ashmansworth** (Ha) — the last two including, respectively, the personal names Rîcmǣr and Ascmēr.

Related terminations, with the same meaning, are *-worthy*, frequently found in Devon and Cornwall, and *-wardine*, common in the West Midlands. Examples of the first are **Fernworthy**, **Thornworthy**, **Highworthy**, **Langworthy**, **Widworthy** and **Smallworthy**, all in Devon and all self-explanatory. At **Wringford** (Co) and **Wringworthy** (Dev) there were probably cider presses. **Canworthy** (Co) is 'enclosure with a cairn'; **Curworthy** (Dev) is 'mill enclosure'. First elements are often personal names, especially in Devon: **Blatchworthy** (Blæcci), **Woolfardisworthy** (Wulfheard), **Holsworthy** (Heald) and **Wilsworthy** (Wifel) all include the names of Anglo-Saxons, as do **Elworthy** (So) and **Chilsworthy** (Co); post-Conquest personal names occur in **Derworthy** (Dev) and **Stroxworthy** (Dev), showing that *worthy* was still alive at the end of the Anglo-Saxon period.

The west midland *-wardine* has variants elsewhere, e.g. in **Worden** and **Worthen** (Dev), which may be compared with **Worthin** (Sa). **Cheswardine** (Sa) is 'cheese enclosure', **Bredwardine** (He/H&W) 'enclosure on a hillside', **Stanwardine** (Sa) 'stone enclosure' and **Ruardean** (Gl) 'enclosure by a hill'. **Northenden** (Ch/GM) — 'north enclosure') was *Norwordine* in Domesday Book. **Ellardine** (Sa), **Ingardine** (Sa), **Pedwardine** (He/H&W) and **Tolladine** (Wo/H&W) are all compounded with personal names.

By far the most common Old English element is *tūn*, 'farm, estate'. Unlike *worth*, this element never occurs alone; it is rare as a first element, **Tonbridge** (K) being a possible case, though the first element here may be the personal name Tunna. Very common indeed are *-tūn* names compounded with *north-*, *west-*, etc, as in the many instances of **Norton, Sutton, Weston** and **Easton, Aston** or **Eston**. This is good evidence that these are not the oldest names in the locality: **Sutton Coldfield** (Wa/WM) (. . . 'in open country where charcoal was burnt') is 'south village' by reference to Lichfield; **King's Norton** (Wa/WM) is so described as being north of (and therefore established after) **Bromsgrove** (Wo/H&W — 'Brēme's grove', first recorded nearly three centuries earlier). Some villages with *-tūn* names may be above others — hence the many examples of **Upton** — or below them, as in the many instances of **Netherton** (La/Mer, Nb, Wo/H&W,

WRY/WYk, Tsd). They may be old or new, attractive in summer or tolerable in winter, noteworthy as possessing a church or a mill, or famous for a product: **Naunton** (Gl), **Newtown** (Gl, Ha, Nb, Wt), the frequent **Newton** and **Newington** and **Newnton** (W) contrast with **Oulton** (Ch, St). **Somerton** (L, Nf, Oxf, So) and **Winterton** (Nf) evidently had seasonal qualities; **Chirton** (Nb/T&W, W), **Cheriton** (Dev, Ha, K, So) and **Cherington** (Wa) were distinguished from neighbouring villages or hamlets by having churches. **Millington** (Ch, ERY/Hum) and **Milton** in several counties had mills. Other places called **Milton**, however, were situated 'in the middle', amongst these being **Milton Bryan** (Bd), **Milton Abbas** (Do), **Milton Keynes** (Bk) and **Milton Malsor** (Nth). **Butterton** (St), **Honiton** (Dev, in South Molton) and **Honington** (Wa) produced butter and honey. The first element in the parish name **Honiton** (Dev), however, is a personal name.

This element is often combined with personal names, the 'dithematic' type being particularly common in the Midlands: **Edgbaston** (Wa/WM), **Osmaston** (Db), **Darlaston** (St, St/WM) and **Kinvaston** (St) celebrate Ecgbald, Osmund, Dēorlāf and Cynewald. The woman's name Cēngifu is found in **Kniveton** (Db), **Knayton** (NRY/NYk) and **Kneeton** (Nt). The growing popularity of **Brighton** (ESus) as a resort caused its name to be shortened from *Brighthelmstone* in the early nineteenth century and concealed yet further the Saxon personal name, Beorhthelm, its first element. Post-Conquest names also occur: **Bryanston** (Do) preserves the memory of Brian de Insula, who lived in the thirteenth century; **Cripstone** (Co) commemorates Henry Cryspyn (1356); **Flamston** (W) has as its first element the name of Walter Flambard (1202).

References to natural features include some to brooks, in **Brockton** (Sa), **Brotton** (NRY/Clev) and **Broughton** (Bk, Cu/Cba, Db, La). A marsh is referred to in **Marston** and **Merston** (frequent), a lake in **Merton** (Sr/GL, Dev, Nf, Oxf) and a wood in **Wootton** (frequent) or **Wotton** (Bk, Gl). The names of domestic and wild animals or cultivated and wild plants occur in **Calverton** (Nt), **Lambton** (Du), **Oxton** (Ch/Mer), **Shepton** (So), **Skipton** (WRY/NYk), **Foxton** (Lei), **Flaxton** (NRY/NYk), **Linton** (He/H&W), **Ryton** (Du/T&W), **Brereton** (St), **Nettleton** (L) **Rushton** (Ch) and **Lemington** (Nb/T&W) — the last referring to the speedwell, *hleomuc* in Old English.

The frequent **Thornton, Appleton** and **Ashton**, **Elmton** (Db), **Pyrton** (Oxf) and **Plumpton** (Cu/Cba) are self-explanatory. **Accrington** (La) is 'acorn farm', almost certainly a pig farm utilising acorns gathered in Rossendale Forest. Oak trees are also alluded to in the many instances of **Acton**, and in **Aikton** (Cu/Cba), **Ackton** (WRY/WYk) and **Aughton** (La, ERY/Hum,

WRY/SYk). **Maperton** (So) and **Mappleton** (Db, ERY/Hum) are 'maple-tree farm'. **Alderton** (Sa, Sf) is 'alder farm', but a personal name (Ealdere) is the first element in **Alderton** (Gl, W, Nth), and in 1062 the same name in Essex was *Ælwartune*, i.e. 'Ælfweard's estate'.

Individual trees served as landmarks indicating boundaries or meeting places. **Braintree** (Ess) is 'Branuc's tree' and **Coventry** (Wa/WM) 'Cōfa's tree'. The term probably has the sense 'wooden (memorial) cross' in **Oswestry** (Sa), associated in legend with the saintly Oswald, killed in battle at an unidentified place thought to have been near here. **Elstree** (Hrt) reached its present form by the misdivision of some such expression as 'at Tidwulf's tree'.

Sometimes the names comment appreciatively or otherwise on the places. **Fairfield** (Db) means 'fine stretch of open country'. **Fairford** (Gl), 'clear ford', contrasts with **Fulford** (freq.). In **Verwood** (Do), the dialect form of 'fair' occurs. But not all apparently derogatory names are to be taken at face value. **Mucking** (Ess), for example, is merely the place occupied by 'the followers of the Muca or Mucca'. The process of naming did not stop with the Anglo-Saxons and the next chapters will show that new waves of invaders and colonists played their own part in modifying or replacing names in the places where they settled.

6. Norsemen and Normans

During the last quarter of the ninth century there was extensive Scandinavian settlement in the north and east of England. A separate wave of invaders came a little later to north-west England — not direct from their homeland but from Ireland, where there had been Scandinavian colonies for about a century. The earlier settlers (those in the east) were mostly Danes; those from Ireland were of Norwegian origin, evidently still speaking their native language, but markedly influenced by the Irish.

As the Scandinavian colonisation was neither so prolonged nor so widespread as the Anglo-Saxon settlement, there are not so many place-names to bear witness to it. Most of these are to be found in the 'Danelaw' (the area to the north and east of Watling Street — roughly a line from London to Chester). Within the Danelaw, the distribution of Scandinavian names is uneven, with heavy concentrations in the North and East Ridings of Yorkshire, the Lake District, Cheshire, Lincolnshire, the East Midlands and East Anglia.

The most common termination of Scandinavian names in England is -*by*, usually rendered as 'village'. Most of these places were settled before the Vikings took them over, and when it is realised that the process was essentially one of *renaming* some of the peculiarities of the names ending in *-by* will be better understood. One of these peculiarities is that the termination is quite often added to an Old English word, e.g. **Utterby** (L), in which the first element is Old English *uterra*, 'outer, more remote'; there is another Lincolnshire name, **Itterby** (now Humberside), in which the first element is the corresponding Old Norse word, *ytri*. What was felt to be a foreign element was replaced by a vernacular word in names like **Newby** (Cu/Cba). The frequent **Ashby** shows a replacement of Old Norse *askr* by Old English *æsc*. In **Asby** (We/Cba) the Scandinavian form remains undisturbed.

Selby (WRY/NYk) is 'village with willows'; **Linby** (Nt) is 'village with lime trees'; **Thrimby** (We/Cba) is 'thorn-bush village'. **Kirkby** or **Kirby**, 'village with a church', is very common in the Danelaw, as also is **Crosby**, 'village with a cross'. **Coningsby** was owned by a king (ON *kunung*), and **Whenby** (NRY/NYk) by women. This ending is frequently added to personal names. These may be Scandinavian, as in **Brumby** (L/Hum), **Ormsby** (NRY/Clev, Nf), **Barkby** (Lei), **Stainsby** (Db), **Bleasby** (Nt), **Humby** (L — found also in Scotland), **Corby** (L, Nth) and **Oadby** (Lei); Irish, as in **Duggleby** (ERY/NYk) and **Lackenby** (NRY/Clev); English, as in **Ellerby** (NRY/NYk) and **Gutterby** (Cu/Cba); or even Norman, as in the Cumberland (now Cumbria) names **Allonby, Harraby, Moresby, Ponsonby** and **Tarraby**. **Grimsby** (L/Hum), which contains the Scandinavian name Grim, is probably the best known example of this group. **Whitby** (NRY/NYk), 'white village' or, perhaps, 'Hviti's village', replaces the Old English name recorded by Bede, *Streonæshalch* (the meaning of which is uncertain). In **Whitby** (Ch) replacement of a different kind has taken place: its earliest form was *Witeberia*, but Old English *burh* soon gave way to the Scandinavian element. There are 150 names ending in *-by* in the former North Riding alone. **Danby** (NRY/NYk), **Denaby** (WRY/SYk) and **Denby** (Db, WRY/WYk) mean 'village of the Danes'; these names indicate Danish settlements in areas predominantly occupied by other peoples. Their neighbours may have been English, and the use of such a name points to the existence of a living Anglo-Scandinavian dialect in the area concerned. Similar names are **Normanby** (L, L/Hum, NRY/Clev, NRY/NYk), 'Norwegians' village', **Firsby** (L), **Frisby** (Lei), 'Frisians' village', **Ingleby** (Db, L, NRY/NYk), 'village of the English', and **Birkby** (Cu/Cba), 'village of the Britons'. **Irby** (Ch/Mer), 'village of the Irishmen', shows replacement of Old English *burh* as in the Cheshire Whitby. The Frenchman referred to in **Frankby** (Ch/Mer) is mentioned in Domesday Book, though the place itself is not included.

The element *thorp*, very common in Scandinavian names, has to be distinguished from the Old English element found in such names as **Althorp** (Nth), 'Olla's village'. Both modern spellings and local pronunciation can be of help: names derived from Old English *throp* are often pronounced 'throp' though many compounds containing this element end in *-thorp(e)*. There is little doubt about the simple forms **Thrope** (WRY/NYk), **Throope** (W) and **Thrupp** (Brk/Oxf, Gl, Nth, Oxf). Compounds include **Astrop** (Nth, 'eastern village'), **Southrop(e)** (Gl, Oxf), **Westrip** (Gl) and **Westrop** (W). The memorable **Adlestrop** (Gl) is 'Tatel's village', which shows a spelling development similar to that of Elstree. In **Aston Upthorpe** (Brk/Oxf), the 'higher village' of Aston, the early form *Upthrop* indicates clearly the Old English element.

The Scandinavian term means 'secondary settlement' and often follows the name of the parent village, e.g. **Barkby Thorpe** (Lei), **Tattershall Thorpe** (L), **Scotton Thorpe** (WRY/NYk) and **Welwick Thorpe** (ERY/Hum). When compass names are used, they indicate the position of the daughter settlement relative to the original village, e.g. **Easthorpe** and **Westhorpe** (Nt) are the eastern and western dependencies of Southwell. In **Littlethorpe** (WRY/NYk), **Newthorpe** (Nt, WRY/NYk), **Woodthorpe** (WRY/SYk), **Milnthorpe** (Nt, We/Cba, WRY/WYk), **Kingthorpe** (L) and **Bishopthorpe** (WRY/NYk) the specifiers are all Old English and self-explanatory, whereas **Coneysthorpe** (NRY/NYk) and **Skinnerthorpe** (WRY/SYk) have as their first elements the Old Norse *kunung*, 'king', and *skinnari*, 'skinner'.

Thorp is very frequently combined with Old Norse personal names, as in **Alethorpe** (Nf), **Caythorpe** (ERY/Hum), **Grimethorpe** (WRY/SYk), **Kettlethorpe** (WRY/WYk) and **Sibthorpe** (Nt). **Streetthorpe** (WRY/SYk) has no connection with a Roman road (as is usually signified by names containing *Street, Strat* or *Stret*) but is derived from the Old Norse personal name Styr. **Oakthorpe** (Lei) is also deceptive as it commemorates a Scandinavian called Aki; **Bromkinsthorpe** (Lei) (*Bruneskinnestorp* in 1233) has as its first element the Scandinavian nickname *Brunskinn*, 'one with brown skin'. *Thorpe* names continued to be formed after the Norman Conquest, for example **Countesthorpe** (Lei), which includes a title of nobility unknown to the Anglo-Saxons, **Donisthorpe** (Lei), containing the Old French personal name Durand, and **Painsthorpe** (ERY/Hum), which has as its first element the Middle English personal name Pain, found also (but with an English termination) in **Painswick** (Gl).

The meanings 'clearing in a forest, meadow, paddock' are assigned to *thveit*, another very common element in names of Scandinavian origin in the north of England. There may be prefixed to this a variety of qualifiers, such as adjectives relating to size, shape, etc., as in **Braithwaite** (Cu/Cba), **Micklethwaite** (Cu/Cba, WRY/WYk), **Langthwaite** (Cu/Cba), NRY/NYk) and **Smaithwaite** (Cu/Cba) — respectively clearings that are broad, great, long, and small or narrow. Tree names occur in **Applethwaite** (Cu/Cba), **Hawthornthwaite** (La), **Thornthwaite** (Cu/Cba, We/Cba, WRY/NYk) and **Birthwaite** (WRY/SYk), the last alluding to the birch tree. Names of wild and cultivated plants are found in **Brackenthwaite** (Cu/Cba, WRY/NYk), and **Bruthwaite** (Cu/Cba — 'briar clearing'). Less easy to identify are **Slaithwaite** (WRY/WYk), 'sloe clearing', **Seathwaite** (Cu/Cba), 'sedge clearing', **Haverthwaite** (La/Cba), 'oats clearing', **Linethwaite** (Cu/Cba), 'flax clearing', and **Thackthwaite** (Cu/Cba, WRY/Cba), 'clearing where thatching material was obtained'. A rare Midlands example occurs in **Huthwaite** (Nt), 'clearing on a hill-spur'. More than ten per cent of first elements consist of personal names, as in **Austhwaite** (Cu/Cba), **Finsthwaite** (La/Cba), **Hampsthwaite** (WRY/NYk), **Yockenthwaite** (WRY/NYk) and **Wickerthwaite** (Cu/Cba).

The Scandinavian way of life is commemorated in many place-names. Social, political and legal organisations can be detected in names like **Holderness** (ERY/Hum), '*hold's* promontory', and **Dringhoe** (ERY/Hum), '*dreng's* mound', which allude to two of the orders in Viking society: the *hold*, or yeoman, and the *dreng*, or free tenant. The *leysingi* ('freedman') is alluded to in **Lazenby** (NRY/Clev, NRY/NYk), **Lazonby** (Cu/Cba) and **Lazencroft** (WRY/WYk). The term *bondi* ('free landowner'), possibly occurring in **Bonby** (L/Hum), is one of a number of elements difficult to distinguish from common Scandinavian personal names.

Scandinavian public assemblies are alluded to in **Fingay Hill** (NRY/NYk) — *thing-haugr*, 'assembly mound' — and the former name of **Hangar Hill** (Nt), *Thinghowe*. The Tynwald, or Isle of Man parliament, is so called from the Scandinavian custom of holding such assemblies in an appropriate field, known as *thing-vollr*, which is the origin also of **Thingwall** (Ch/Mer) and, in Scotland, of **Dingwall** (Ross/Hld), **Tingwall** (She) and **Tinewald** (Dmf/D&G).

Of the many names of mixed origin, there is room for only a small selection here. Apart from the replacement of an Old English name by one of Scandinavian origin, as in **Derby** (Db) and **Whitby** (NRY/NYk), it often happened that Old English *-tūn* was added to a Norse personal name, as in the Leicestershire names of **Thurcaston, Thurlaston** and **Thurmaston**, which contain respectively the Scandinavian names Thorketil, Thorleif and Thormod, **Gonalston** (Nt — from Gunnulf) and **Kedleston** (Db — from Ketil). There are so many examples of **Grimston**

(Lei, Nf, Nt, Sf, ERY/Hum, NRY/NYk) that these mixed names are often called 'Grimston hybrids'. Studies have found that places bearing this name are on sites which compare unfavourably with those of villages nearby, and it has even been suggested that the Grim alluded to was the Devil.

In some hybrid names the Norse element comes first. In **Stainley** (WRY/NYk — 'stony glade or clearing') Old English *stān* has given way to the corresponding Old Norse *steinn*, 'stone'. In **Rawcliffe** (NRY/NYk — 'red cliff'), Old English *rēad* has been replaced by Old Norse *rauthr*; the usual development of *Readeclife*, which is an actual early form of this name, is **Radcliffe** (La/GM, Lei, Nt), **Ratcliff** (Mx/GL) or **Redcliff** (So/Av). The modern form of **Broadholme** (Nt) suggests a compound of Old English *brād*, 'broad', and Old Norse *holmr*, 'island in marshes, well-watered land'; but the spellings with *-o-* in *Brodeholm*, 1086, and *Brodholm(e)*, 1200, 1202, show that the first element is the Scandinavian personal name Broddi. The second element has been replaced in **Beckwith** (WRY/NYk), **Bubwith** (ERY/Hum) and **Badby** (Nth); the early forms for these were *Becwudu*, 'beech wood', *Bubbewych*, 'Bubba's outlying farm', and *Baddanbyrig*, 'Badda's fort'. Old Norse *-by* has been substituted for Old English *-burh* also in **Rugby** (Wa), 'Hrōca's fortified place'.

The Scandinavians of north-west England brought with them from Ireland certain linguistic features which appear in the place-names of the area, such as the Old Irish word *airigh*, 'shieling', found in **Arrowe** (Ch/Mer), **Ar.as** (ERY/Hum), **Eryholme** (NRY/NYk), **Argam** (ERY/Hum) and **Arram** (ERY/Hum). Shielings were not only the mountain pastures used in summer, but also the huts occupied by the herdsmen throughout the season. Such shelters could be made with turf — hence **Torver** (La/Cba) — or brushwood, as in **Tirrill** (We/Cba), or stout poles *(stafn)*, alluded to in **Stephney** (Cu/Cba). They might be situated on a precipice (ON *bjarg*), as **Berrier** (Cu/Cba) evidently was; near a mossy bog, like **Mosser** (Cu/Cba) and **Mozergh** (We/Cba); in the middle, as was **Medlar** (La); or in a windy, exposed position, like **Winder** (Cu/Cba, We/Cba). Often the first element is an Old Norse or Old Irish personal name, as in **Anglezarke** (La), **Battrix** (WRY/La), **Mansergh** (We/Cba) and **Goosnargh** (La).

The so-called 'inversion compounds' are also a feature of the naming habits of the colonists of north-west England. Personal names normally occur as the first element in non-Celtic compounds, as has already been seen. In some place-names of this area, however, e.g. **Kirkandrews** (Cu/Cba — three examples), **Kirkoswald** (Cu/Cba), **Aspatria** (Cu/Cba — 'Patrick's ash') and **Seat Sandal** (We/Cba — 'Sandolf's shieling'), the

Celtic usage prevails and the personal name comes second.

It was not only the British Isles that received the attentions of the Vikings; among other places, northern France was also raided by them and subsequently colonised. The province on which they concentrated received, as a result, the name Normandy, 'land of the Northmen'. The Norman Conquest of Britain was, therefore, yet another incursion of Scandinavians. In the meantime Norse had ceased to be the vernacular of these men and when they came to Britain they were speaking a dialect of French, stubbornly denying even the ability to pronounce the tongue of their grandfathers. The name of King Cnut, for instance, became Canute to the Normans, and place-names underwent a similar mutilation. Initial *s* was a difficulty when immediately followed by another consonant: **Tutbury** (St) has been deprived of its first sound, being 'Stut's fortress', and **Nottingham** is what the Normans made of *Snotingaham*. Consonant clusters were simplified or altered in **Durham** (from *Dunholm* by way of *Durelme* and *Dureaume*) and **Cambridge** (from *Grantebrige*). **Diss** (Nf) might be *Ditch* today if the invaders had been able to pronounce the final sound as the Anglo-Saxons did. Similarly, **Leicester, Exeter, Worcester**, etc, have lost the *-ch-* sound found impossible by the Normans. Many of the changes were temporary, and modern forms of some names resemble their Old English progenitors more closely than do the spellings of Domesday Book.

Besides sounds that they evidently regarded as ugly or unpronounceable, the Normans also rejected some English names which contained elements that were distasteful to them. The Essex place called frankly by the Anglo-Saxons *Fulepit*, 'filthy hole', was ennobled by the newcomers into **Beaumont**, 'fair hill' — hardly a translation of the former name, but perhaps there is a touch of irony here. **Belgrave** (Lei) replaced the earlier *Merdegrave*, which the Normans refused to believe meant 'martens' grove'. In Lincolnshire a place known as *Helgelo* ('Helgi's meadow') was renamed **Belleau**, 'fair water'.

The Normans had an eye for fine scenery, as the names beginning with *Beau-* or *Bel-* testify, but a note of disapproval is occasionally sounded, as in **Malzeard** (WRY/NYk), derived from Old French *mal assart*, 'bad clearing'. **Malpas** (Ch), 'difficult passage', is another of these disparaging terms. Because the names designated the sites of castles rather than settlements a place commanding a fine view would be commended as much for military as for aesthetic reasons, and laudatory names are in the great majority, with *Beau-* or *Bel-* in the modern forms. The Old French pronunciation of this element was closer to 'bew', a sound that survives in many names, e.g. **Beaulieu** (Ha), 'fair place', variants of which are the Scottish **Beauly** (Inv/Hld),

Bewdley (Wo/H&W) and **Bewley Castle** (We/Cba). The pronunciation 'bee' is given to the first syllable of **Belvoir** (Lei), 'fine view', **Beamish** (Du), 'fine mansion', and **Beauchief** (Db/SYk), 'fine headland'; another instance is found in **Beachy Head** (ESus), the second word of which is superfluous. **Belper** (Db), **Bearpark** (Du) and **Beaurepair** (Gl) mean 'fair retreat'; **Belasis** (Du/Clev, near Billingham), **Bellasis** (Du, near Durham City), **Bellasize** (ERY/Hum) and **Belsize** (Hrt, Mx/GL, Nth/C) are the different forms now taken by *Bel assis*, 'beautiful seat'.

Beaumont (Cu/Cba) has the pronunciation 'bee-', but **Beaumont** (Ess, La) has the sound 'bo' in the first syllable; all these are 'fine hill'. As Beaumont is common in France some examples may be transferred and not intended to describe the English site. Impressive rather than pretty scenery seems to be alluded to in **Beaufront** (Nb), 'fine brow', and **Beaudesert** (St), 'fine wilderness'. **Beauvale** (Nt) and **Beaumanor** (Lei) are self-explanatory. Not all *Beau-* names are from French; **Beausale** (Wa), for instance, is 'Bēaw's nook of land', **Beaufield** (K) 'Bēaw's open land', and **Beauworth** (Ha) 'bee enclosure'.

Other wholly French names include **Richmond** (NRY/NYk), 'rich hill'. This name, like a number of others, was used in imitation of identical names in France but later was itself used in the renaming of a place in Surrey (now in GL) — **Richmond-upon-Thames**, which until then had been known as *Sheen*, 'shelters'. Monasteries, such as **Grosmont** (NRY/NYk, Mon/Gt), 'big mountain', were sometimes named after their mother houses in France. **Charterhouse on Mendip** (So) is from Chartreuse, the original Carthusian monastery. **Jervaulx** and **Rievaulx** (both NRY/NYk) seem to be translations of the English names 'valley of the river Ure' and 'valley of the river Rye' respectively. **Haltemprice** (ERY/Hum), another monastic name, means 'high enterprise'; the same first element occurs in the hybrid name **Haltwhistle** (Nb), 'high river confluence', and in **Ault Hucknall** (Db), 'high part of Hucca's nook'. **Pontefract** (WRY/WYk) was a renaming of *Tateshale*, 'Tadda's nook of land'; the alternative form of this name is **Pomfret**, which is closer to the traditional pronunciation of the name. The Old French name, *Pontfreit*, 'broken bridge', arose on the establishment of a Cluniac priory and the building of a castle by Ilbert de Lacy, whose estates formed the Honour of Pontefract. The Old French name was latinised (as was customary) in legal documents to *Fractuspons* or *Pons Fractus*. From frequently used forms like *Pontefracto*, 'at Pomfret', the present name resulted, and so it came about that the spelling was derived from Latin, but the spoken form from French. The bridge has been identified as the predecessor of Bubwith Bridge, across a small stream called the Wash Dike.

In **Leafield** (Oxf) the French definite article has been modified to look like a plausible English first element. The site, an open space in Wychwood Forest, would have been 'field' in the earliest sense of the term — an area of felled trees. In early documents it was written *la Feld* or *le Feild*. In names like **Hamble-le-Rice** (Ha), 'Hamble in the brushwood', the French article is a remnant of the phrase *en le*, as in **Chapel-en-le-Frith** (Db), 'chapel in the woodland'. Places on Roman roads receive this treatment quite often, *-le-Street* being suffixed to mean 'on the Roman road'. Examples are **Appleton-le-Street** (NRY/NYk), **Chester-le-Street** (Du) and **Wharram-le-Street** (ERY/NYk). Other suffixes are found in **Bolton le Sands** (La), **Hutton le Hole** (NRY/NYk) and **Burgh le Marsh** (L). Some of the main components in these names must be explained: **Hamble** is a river name meaning 'crooked', **Wharram** is 'enclosure in kettle-shaped valley', and **Bolton** 'estate by dwellings'.

The termination *-ville* does not indicate a Norman origin. Some names with this element are recent, e.g. **Coalville** (Lei), **Ironville** (Db) and **Waterlooville** (Ha), not forgetting **Ankerville, Barbaraville** and **Jemimaville** in Easter Ross (now Hld) in Scotland. In earlier names it is often a development from Old English *feld*, 'open land', as in **Enville** (St), 'level open land', **Longville** (Sa), 'long piece of open land', and **Turville** (Bk), which, like **Therfield** (Hrt), is derived from Old English *thyrre feld*, 'dry open land'. Though the manorial affixes are Norman in the following, the settlement names to which they are added are Scandinavian or English: **Thorpe Satchville** (Lei), **Orton Longueville** and **Waterville** (Hu/C), **Coatham Mundeville** (Du), **Thorpe Mandeville** (Nth), **Weston Colville** (C) and **Aston Flamville** (Lei) retain the names of feudal lords who were granted the manors of Thorpe, Orton ('farm on a riverbank'), Coatham ('place at the cottages'), Weston and Aston. Names of this type are discussed in greater detail in the next chapter.

7. Feudal and manorial names

About ninety-eight per cent of current English place-names originated before 1500, and most of the names now to be examined came into existence between the Norman Conquest and that date. The genius of the Normans was expressed in a unique way in many of the place-names which they generated. Names like **Leighton Buzzard** (Bd), **Eaton Constantine** (Sa), **Eaton Bray** (Bd), **Sydenham Damerel** (Dev), **Stansted Mountfitchet** (Ess), **Ashby de la Zouch** (Lei) and **Upton Scudamore** (W) never fail to impress but often seem obscure. The reason for this is that the second word of these duplex forms is a family-name hardly ever found in other place names, or, if it occurs, it is subtly changed. It records the tenure of a manor by a medieval noble and his descendants. Other names of this type allude to lordships held by feudal officers and ecclesiastical dignitaries. Perhaps it was a heightened sense of personal identity which led the Normans to use their family or official names in this way in place-names — not followed by a termination, as the Saxons and Danes preferred, or even following a topographical element (in the Celtic fashion), but normally standing alone and after the existing name, with a kind of aggressive independence.

The association of the Busard family with **Leighton Buzzard** was first recorded in 1254; the addition serves to distinguish this **Leighton** ('leek farm') from a number of others, just as the two instances of **Eaton** are specified by their feudal additions of Constantine (a family from Côtentin in France) and Bray (recalling Sir Reginald Bray, who held the manor in 1490). There are many places called **Eaton** ('estate by a river' or 'estate on a river island') and so distinguishing affixes are useful; there are also **Eaton Tregose** (He/H&W), **Eaton Hastings** (Brk/Oxf) and **Eaton Mascott** (Sa). **Sydenham Damerel** was held by John D'Albemarle in 1242; **Sydenham** here and in some counties means 'broad riverside pasture' (though the Greater London place is 'Cippa's riverside pasture'). The same family name occurs in **Hinton Admiral** (Ha — *Henton Damarle* in 1412). **Hinton** is often 'estate on high land'.

The addition in **Stansted Mountfitchet** (Ess), the lords of which were from Montfiquet in Normandy, helps to distinguish it from **Stanstead Abbots** (Hrt), nearby, and **Stanstead** (Sf). **Stanste(a)d** means 'stone place' and may refer to the remains of Roman villas found in several of them. Roger de la Zuche was the tenant of **Ashby** in 1200; other manorial forms of this fairly common name include **Ashby de la Launde** (L) and **Ashby Folville** (Lei). In one instance — **Mears Ashby** (Nth) — the family name (from Marais in France) is placed first. Godfrey Escudamore came into possession of **Upton** in the mid twelfth century. Again, the basic place-name ('higher village') is a common one, and other manorial affixes are found, as in **Upton Cressett** (Sa), **Upton Warren** (Wo/H&W) and **Upton Lovell** (W). **Waters Upton** (Sa) is another example of the reversal of the usual order, this place being named after Walter Fitzjohn.

Although most manorial titles are first recorded in the twelfth century or later, some are implied in entries in Domesday Book (1086). The earliest record of the affix in **Kingston Bagpuize** (Brk/Oxf) is dated 1284, but the manor was held in 1086 by Ralph de Bagpuize, from Baquepuis in Normandy. **Sutton Waldron** (Do) was held by one Walerannus in 1086, and Osbeorn Gifard is named in Domesday Book as holding the manor now known as **Stoke Gifford** (Gl/Av). Even after the Norman Conquest, Queen Edith, widow of Edward the Confessor, retained her estates, which included **Stoke Edith** (He/H&W) and **Edith Weston** (R/Lei). **Marks Tey** (Ess, 'enclosure held by de Merck') was previously *Teye de Mandevill*; its lord was Geoffrey de Mandeville in 1086. **Tooting Bec** (Sr/GL) was first so called in 1255, but it was described in 1086 as held by the Abbey of *Bech*, i.e. Bec-Hellouin in Normandy. The other manor in Tooting ('Tota's people'), Lower (or South) Tooting, known also as **Tooting Graveney**, was held by Richard de Gravenel in 1215; he is thought to have derived his surname from Graveney in Kent.

In Bedfordshire a common name meaning 'aspen-tree wood' is set off with a Norman family name in **Aspley Guise**, commemorating the local lord in 1276. **Houghton Conquest**, in the same county, bears an even more resounding addition. The Conquest family was first recorded as associated with this place, 'farm on a spur of land', in 1223. The Oxfordshire name **Berrick Salome** has an exotic, even biblical, ring to it. **Berrick** (like the more frequent **Berwick**), 'barley farm', usually refers to a small dependency of a large estate. The addition alludes to the family of Almaric de Suleham, 1235, named from **Sulham** ('village in a narrow valley') in the neighbouring county of Berkshire. The same family held **Britwell Salome** (Oxf); a second manor of **Britwell** ('bright spring'), **Britwell Prior**, was in the hands of the prior of Christchurch, Canterbury, who also held the other Berrick manor, **Berrick Prior**.

The fairly common **Wootton** ('farm by a wood') often receives manorial affixes. **Wootton Basset** (W), **Wooton Courtney** (So) and **Wootton Fitzpaine** (Do) record connections with those great families; a more venerable example is **Wootton Wawen** (Wa), traceable to a pre-Conquest owner, Wagene de Wotton, mentioned in 1050. Names spelt **Wotton** (with the same meaning) have descriptive additions rather than feudal ones, e.g. **Wotton Underwood** (Bk, 'below a wood' — namely Bernwood Forest') and **Wotton under Edge** (Gl, 'at the foot of a hill').

Easton is another common name distinguished by manorial additions, e.g. **Easton Grey, Easton Bassett** and **Easton Percy** (all in Wiltshire), **Easton Bavents** (Sf) and **Easton Maudit** (Nth). The last surname, found also in **Hartley Mauditt** (Ha), is one of the candid nicknames both the Vikings and Normans were fond of; it means 'badly educated'. **Herstmonceux** (ESus) and **Hurstpierpoint** (WSus) differ from most feudal place-names by being single words in their modern form. Old English *hyrst*, found also in **Hirst** (Nb) and **Hirst Courtney** (WRY/NYk), means 'wooded hill'. The Monceux family, who held their manor from the twelfth century, took their name from Monceaux, in Calvados,

Normandy; the Pierpoints were senior, however, since Robert de Pierpoint held his *Herst* at the time of the Domesday Book. Other examples of names in which the feudal element is impacted with the basic name are **Stogumber** and **Stogursey** (So). The common name **Stoke** ('special or holy place') is in the first name supplemented by Gumer or Gunner. **Storgursey** was held during the reign of Henry I by William de Curci, a noble whose family came from Courcy in Normandy. In addition to **Stoke Edith** (He/H&W), already discussed, many other places called **Stoke** are distinguished in this way. **Stoke Abbot** (Do) was held by the Abbot of Sherborne; **Stoke Albany** (Nth) was a territory of the family taking its name from the Norman place Aubigny. The family named in **Stoke Damarel** (Dev) is the same as that in **Sydenham Damerel** (Dev) and **Hinton Admiral** (Ha). **Stoke Poges** (Bk), of Gray's *Elegy* fame, was held in 1255 by Hubert le Pugeis.

From some manorial names the place-name component has disappeared, leaving only the feudal element. **Virley** (Ess) was earlier *Salcote Verly*, held by Robert de Verli in 1086; 'salt shed' was perhaps too modest to sustain a lordly addition. This could hardly be said of **Shendish** (Hrt), part of a large settlement at **Langley**; **Kings Langley** and **Abbots Langley** refer to two of the divisions, but *Langeleye Chendut*, held by Ralph Chaineduit in the twelfth century, was already just *Shenduch* or *Chandoys* by the late sixteenth. **Chenies** (Bk) was originally *Isenhamstede* ('Isa's homestead'); the manorial addition of *Cheyne* is found in thirteenth-century documents, and in 1536 *Cheynes* gives us the name almost in its modern form.

Additions are sometimes in Latin. **Zeal Monachorum** (Dev) may suggest a high degree of virtue among its inhabitants. The affix means 'of the monks', namely those of Buckfast Abbey. **Zeal** represents the Old English word *sele*, 'a hall'. At **Buckland Monachorum** (Dev) there was an abbey, and at **Buckland Sororum** (So) ('sisters' Buckland', also known as **Minchin Buckland**, 'nuns' Buckland') a nunnery. **Buckland**, 'land held by charter', occurs mostly in the south of England; other instances with manorial additions include **Buckland Dinham** (So, from de Dinant family) and the Devon places **Buckland Brewer** (held by William Briwerre in the early thirteenth century) and **Egg Buckland** (alluding to a pre-Conquest owner, a Saxon called Heca). **Ashby Puerorum** (L) was assigned for the benefit of the choir boys of Lincoln Cathedral, a purpose alluded to in a 1291 form, *Askeby parvorum chori Lincolniensis*.

Latin additions often relate to ecclesiastical ownership, but this does not completely explain the continued use of forms appropriate to medieval documents. Many such documents were in Latin — at one time, indeed, most were — and descriptive terms added to place-names were frequently translated or otherwise transformed in deeds of property. Latin was used in church but it was not exclusively churchmen who had occasion to refer to the names of their manors. *Esseby Canonicorum* has not survived in that form but has become **Canons Ashby** (Nth); both additions allude to the priory of Augustinian canons founded there in the twelfth century. Similarly, *Deverel Monachorum* (a possession of Glastonbury Abbey) is now **Monkton Deverill** (W), the basic name being of British origin, 'upland fertile land by a stream'.

However, many surviving Latin affixes are in names associated with the church. **Cerne Abbas** and **Milton Abbas** (Do) were monastic manors; **Compton Abbas** (Do) was an ancient possession (from about 871) of Shaftesbury Abbey; the name here means 'abbess's Compton, i.e. village in a narrow valley'. **Compton Abbas West** (Do), however, is 'abbot's Compton', being a possession of Milton Abbey. **Toller Fratrum** (Do), 'Toller of the brethren', was owned by Forde Abbey; **Toller Porcorum** (Do), 'Toller of the pigs', was evidently noteworthy in that respect. They are both on a river formerly called *Toller*, probably 'stream in a deep valley'. **Whitchurch Canonicorum** (Do), 'canons' Whitchurch, i.e., white (stone) church', was the possession of a Norman abbey.

Bishops are alluded to in **Wick Episcopi** (Wo/H&W), belonging to the Bishop of Worcester, and in **Huish Episcopi** and **Kingsbury Episcopi** (So), both possessions of the Bishop of Bath and Wells. **Huish** means 'household (land)' and is probably equivalent to 'hide'. In **Kingsbury Regis** (So), the affix, meaning 'of the king', seems superfluous, as the name itself means 'royal manor', but it distinguishes the estate retained by the king from that granted to the bishop, just as the additions in **Kings Langley** and **Abbots Langley** (Hrt) and **Kings Bromley** and **Abbots Bromley** (St) discriminate between royal and monastic lands. The affix *Regis* is found also in **Rowley Regis** (St/WM), **Bere Regis**, **Melcombe Regis** and **Lyme Regis** (Do). The royal connection with **Salcombe Regis** (Dev) is obscure, but in **Bognor Regis** (WSus) the addition is honorific rather than manorial, having been bestowed by King George V in acknowledgement of the quality of the place in restoring him to health in 1929.

Other Latin additions, apart from manorial ones, include the fairly common *Magna* and *Parva*, 'great' and 'little', used to distinguish two places of the same name, e.g. **Ash Magna** and **Parva** (Sa), **Appleby Magna** and **Parva** (Lei) and **Ashby Magna** and **Parva** (Lei). Not only are **Wigston Magna** and **Parva** (Lei) a considerable distance apart, they are also of different origins; **Wigston Magna** was formerly *Wichingestone*, 'the Viking's village', and **Wigston Parva** *Wicgestan*, 'Wicga's stone'. *Ambo*, 'both', is used of a union of two parishes bearing the same name; **Wendens Ambo** (Ess) comprises **Great** and **Little Wenden**, 'place on a winding stream'; **Fulfords Ambo** (ERY/NYk) unites **Gate Fulford** (on the York to Doncaster road) and **Water Fulford** (beside the river Ouse). The affix in **Ryme Intrinseca** (Do) means 'within the bounds' and relates to the position of a parish relative to a town.

In **Walton Inferior** and **Superior** (Ch) Latin forms replace the more usual 'Lower' and 'Upper'. Latin prepositions are used in **Norton juxta Twycross** (Lei), **Langar cum Barnstone** (Nth), **Stratford sub Castle** (W) and **Weston in Gordano** (So/Av), the connectives meaning, respectively, 'near', 'with', 'under' and 'in'. The last name, like **Easton in Gordano**, has an addition consisting of a Latinised phrase, **Gordano** being originally Old English *gara denu*, 'valley in a *gore* or triangle of land'. This term is also found in **Kensington Gore** (Mx/GL). The Latin phrase in **Weston super Mare** (So/Av) tells us that the town is 'on the sea'. **Blandford Forum** (Do) is 'Blandford with a market'. *Forum* is equivalent to the first word in **Chipping Norton** (Oxf); indeed, one early form of the Dorset name, which means 'ford where gudgeon could be caught', was *Cheping Blaneford* (1288). The Latin affix in **Barton in Fabis** (Nt) is a translation of that in **Barton in the Beans** (Lei); **Barton**, 'corn farm', is the fairly common term for an outlying grange or subsidiary farm on the estate.

8. Place-names in Wales and the Isle of Man

Though the linguistic threads among the place-names of Wales are not so tangled as those of England or Scotland, a Welsh map presents a number of rewarding features. There are many Celtic names, but there are not a few English ones also; others are of Scandinavian origin, and some look Welsh but are really English (e.g. **Prestatyn**, Clw) or partly English (e.g. **Rhyl**, Clw).

The Old English word *Wealas*, 'Celtic-speaking strangers, foreigners', is an element in a number of place-names, e.g. **Walton** (frequent) and **Walworth** (Du, Sr/GL), respectively 'estate' and 'enclosure' of the Britons. **Wales** (WRY/SYk) was probably a British settlement among Angles. The Welsh call themselves *Cymry* and their country *Cymru* — modern orthographic variants of a name derived from the Brittonic *Combrugi* meaning 'people from the same territory'.

The name of the capital, **Cardiff (Caerdydd)** (SGlam, 'fort on the river'), contains the element *caer*, which reflects the turbulent history of medieval Wales. **Caerllion (Caerleon-on-Usk)** (Gt, 'fort of the legions'), retains a memory of Roman occupation. Welsh *llion* represents Latin *legionum*, 'of the legions', a term which also appears in medieval references to **Chester**. Just as the latter name was modified in its English form, by dropping its first element *Lega* and thus avoiding confusion with **Leicester**, so **Caerleon** had to be differentiated from the Welsh form of **Chester**, which was also *Caerlleon*. Accordingly *ar-Wysg*, 'on Usk', was added.

Caernarvon (Caernarfon) (Gd) means 'fortress in Arfon, i.e. facing Anglesey'. **Carmarthen** (Dyf) is also a *Caer-* name — **Caerfyrddin** in Welsh — 'fort at *Maridunum*, i.e. the sea fort'. This tautological name contains two elements (one ancient, one recent) meaning 'fort'. **Caerphilly** (MGlam) is the anglicised spelling of **Caerffili**, 'Ffili's stronghold'. The spelling with *-ph-* is not a fanciful restoration by eighteenth-century antiquarians but dates from as early as 1314. **Aberteifi**, 'mouth of the river Teifi' is better known to English-speaking travellers as **Cardigan** (Dyf); this is not a *Caer-* name but is from the regional name *Ceredigion*, 'land of Ceredig'.

Swansea (WGlam) is a deceptive name. It is not English, though few would think it Welsh, but of Scandinavian origin and means 'Sveinn's island', alluding to a former islet in the Tawe ('dark river') estuary; the Welsh name for Swansea refers to this location — **Abertawe**. Also of English appearance but of Norse origin is **Milford Haven** (Dyf), 'sandy inlet', from Old Norse *melr*, 'sandbank', and in which the *-ford* element, as in the Irish names **Waterford** and **Wexford**, represents Old Norse *fjorthr*. **Haven** was added when *fjorthr*, no longer understood, had been 'normalised' to *-ford*. Also unnecessary is *Island* suffixed to **Caldy** (Dyf), 'cold island' or 'island of the springs', and to **Grassholm** and **Skokholm** (both Dyf), respectively 'grass island' and 'island by a deep channel'.

The main part of the name **Haverfordwest** (Dyf) is Scandinavian and means 'ford used by goats'. *West* was added in about 1409, to distinguish this name from Hereford. **Fishguard** (Dyf) is derived from Old Norse *fiskr-garthr*, 'fish enclosure'. It was the Scandinavian custom to preserve live fish in enclosed pools on the sea-shore, so that they could be taken easily as required. **Fistard** (IOM) is of similar origin.

English speakers refer to the island known in Welsh as **Môn** ('mountain') by its Scandinavian name, **Anglesey**, 'Ongull's island'. It contains some place-names of great interest. **Holyhead (Caer Gybi)** means 'holy headland'; the Welsh name ('Cybi's stronghold') refers to the saint who made this such a famous ecclesiastical settlement. **Beaumaris** aptly bears the Norman descriptive name of 'beautiful marsh' as its site was once marshland. Norse names are found for maritime features, e.g. **North** and **South Stack** and the rocky islets, **The Skerries**.

On Anglesey also is situated perhaps the only place whose name has been used as a tourist attraction. **Llanfairpwllgwyngyll** (or even Llanfair P.G.) is sufficient for normal purposes. A record-breaking addition of nearly forty more letters was devised by a local humorist. The full name, as it appears on the signs at the railway station, is **Llanfairpwllgwyngyllgogerychwyrndro-bwllllandysiliogogogoch**. The short version means 'St Mary's church by Pwllgwyngyll, i.e. the white hazel pool'. When the anonymous nineteenth-century joker expanded the name, he ended his monster with the name of the next parish, **Llandysilio**, but in the modified form of the same name applied to a *different* place, in Cardiganshire (now Dyfed), where the parish is combined with its neighbour **Gogo** ('the cave'). The middle section, *goger y chwyrn drobwll*, 'near the fierce whirlpool', alludes to Pwll Ceris in Menai Strait, but is not an authentic place-name. The final syllable, *-goch*, of no local significance, was added perhaps to round off the whole construction, and possibly to signal that it should not be taken seriously. But any record-breaker will take the fancy of the credulous (including the compilers of collections of such things) and it has been said that the hoax has deceived even many Welsh people. A similar prank was played on innocent visitors when a local innkeeper 'explained' the name **Beddgelert** (Gd) as 'grave of Gelert', alluding to the dog said to have been killed by Llewelyn, who thought it had devoured his child. As the name was originally *Bedkelert*, 'Celert's grave', with an Old Irish personal name as the second element, there is no connection with the fictitious beast. The story has been recounted in many places and dates from times long before Llewelyn.

Llan, meaning 'church', occurs in the English border counties, e.g. **Llanymynech** (Sa), 'church of the monks', **Llancillo** (He/ H&W), 'church of St Sulbiu', and **Llandinabo** (He), 'church of Junabui'. The corresponding Cornish *Lan* is found in **Landkey** (Dev), 'church of St Cai', and **Landewednack** (Co), 'church of St Gwennock'. In Wales the element is very frequent indeed, **Llanfair**, 'church of St Mary', being found so often that distinguishing elements are added. **Llanfairfechan** (Gd) means 'little church of St Mary'; **Llanfair Caereinion** (Pws, 'St Mary's church by the fort of Einion'); **Llanfair-ar-y-Bryn** (Dyf, '. . . on the cliff'). In **Llanfair-ym-Muallt** (Pws), the affix, meaning 'in the cow pasture', becomes the main part of the anglicised name, **Builth Wells**, with an addition alluding to the chalybeate springs there. This affix is also found in **Llandrindod Wells** (Pws, 'church of the Holy Trinity'), and in **Llanwrtyd Wells** (Pws, 'church of St Gwrtud'), both places being much favoured spas in the nineteenth century, when *Wells* was affixed to the names.

Llanfihangel, 'church of St Michael', is another name so frequently occurring as to need descriptive additions. **Llanfihangel-y-pwll** (S Glam) is also known as **Michaelston-le-Pit**, which approximately translates the Welsh name. Other church dedications are recorded in **Llandudno** (Gd — St Tudno), **Llangollen** (Clw — St Collen), **Llanelli** (Dyf — St Elli) and **Llandeilo** (Dyf — St Teilo). **Llantrisant** (M Glam) means 'church of three saints' — namely Dyfodwg, Gwynno and Illtud. **Llangefni** (Gd) is 'church by the river Cefni'; **Llandovery** (Dyf, 'church near the waters'), the Welsh form of which is **Llanmyddyfri**. **Llanbedr Pont Steffan**, 'church of St Peter at St Stephen's bridge' is perhaps better known in its anglicised form of **Lampeter** (Dyf). **Llanasa** (Clw) is 'church of St Asaph' but the place called **St Asaph** (Clw) in English is **Llanelwy** in Welsh, from its location on the river of that name. **St David's (Tyddewi)** (Dyf) is, as can be seen, not a *Llan* name; the Welsh form uses the term *ty*, 'house', instead. St David's residence there in a grove is alluded to in the alternative name *Mynyw*, the Latin form of which, *Menevia*, was used for the diocese.

Although *Aber*, 'river mouth', frequently occurs in Welsh names, this prefix is not restricted to Wales (being found also in Scotland). The second element in *Aber-* names is usually the name of the river. **Aberystwyth** (Dyf), 'mouth of the river Ystwyth', describes the site of an early castle rather than that of the modern town, which is on the Rheidol. **Ystwyth** means 'winding river' and occurs also in **Ysbyty Ystwyth** (Dyf), 'hospice on the Ystwyth'. **Abergele** (Clw, 'mouth of the Gele'), includes a river-name meaning 'straight', being literally 'spear'. In **Abergavenny** (Gt) the river-name, of British origin, *Gobannion*, means '(river) used by smiths'. The name of the river in **Aberaeron** (Dyf) is that of the Celtic battle goddess. **Aberdovey** (Gd), the English form of **Aberdyfi**, is an attempt to represent the pronunciation of the Welsh name; **Dyfi** means 'dark'.

The element *pont*, 'bridge', appears in a number of Welsh names. **Pontypridd** (MGlam) means 'bridge of the earthen house'; **Pontnewydd** (Gt) is 'new bridge'; **Pontfaen** (Pws) is 'stone bridge'. Two places are called **Talybont** (Dyf, Gd), meaning 'end of the bridge', corresponding to the Mid Glamorgan **Bridgend** (known in Welsh as **Pen-y-bont**). **Pontarddulais** (W Glam) means 'bridge over the river' **Dulais**, the river-name being of similar origin to a number called **Douglas**, 'black stream'. **Pontypool** (Gt) is 'bridge of the pool', the last element being the English word *pool*.

The former Welsh county names have a variety of origins. Most are Celtic, including some already mentioned as town names: **Caernarvon** (Gd), **Cardigan** (Dyf) and **Carmarthen**

(Dyf). In the extreme south-west is **Pembroke** (Dyf 'end land'). **Glamorgan** is 'Morgan's shore'; **Brecknock (Brecon)** (now Pws) is 'territory of Brychan'; **Merioneth**, 'territory of Meirion'. **Denbigh** (Clw) has the same meaning, 'little fort', as **Tenby** (Dyf). **Montgomery** (Pws) is a feudal name, transferred from the baron's home of Montgommery in Calvados. Both **Flint** (Clw), 'hard rock', and **Radnor** (Pws), 'red hillside', are of English origin; **Monmouth** (Gt), a hybrid as befits a border county, takes its name from the town at the 'mouth of the Mynwy', the river possibly having been given the tribal name, *Menapii*.

Local government reorganisation brought about the revival of some ancient names, though they are applied to areas different in extent from the earlier ones. **Gwynedd** means 'region of the hunters'; **Clwyd** is 'hurdle place', possibly alluding to a ford on the river. **Dyfed** is derived from *Demetae*, a tribal name of unknown origin. **Powys** means 'territory of the dwellers in the open country'; **Gwent** is 'market'. The old county of **Glamorgan** was divided into three: **West, South** and **Mid Glamorgan**.

Tintern (Gt) means 'king's fort', **Rhuthun** (Clw), 'red fort', **Raglan** (Gt) 'rampart' and **Harlech** (Gd) 'fair slab of stone', so called before the castle was constructed on this commanding crag. **Ffestiniog** (Gd) is 'defence territory, stronghold', **Blaenau Ffestiniog** (Gd) being the 'heights' above it. In South Wales **Blaenau** (Gt) was earlier known as *Blaenau Gwent*. **Rhuddlan** (Clw) is the 'red bank' of the river Clwyd. **Bangor** is found twice in Wales (Clw, Gd) and occurs also in County Down; the name, meaning 'crossbar in hurdle', probably alludes to the enclosing fence of a monastery. **Dolgellau** (Gd), 'meadow of the cells', may also refer to a monastery. **Betws-y-coed** (Gd) means 'prayer house in the wood'. **Merthyr Tydfil** (MGlam) is 'grave of St Tudful'. **Bala** (Gd) means 'outlet from a lake', and **Pwllheli** (Gd), 'salt pools'. **Bethesda** (Gd, Dyf) is one of the many biblical names given to nineteenth-century chapels, later being applied to settlements growing up around the places of worship.

Town names of English origin include **Newtown** (Pws), **Middletown** (Pws) and **Newport** (Gt, Dyf), all of which are self-explanatory. **Hawarden** (Clw) is 'high enclosure', the second element of which is *worthign*, frequent in the adjoining English counties. The Welsh name is **Penarlâg**, 'height of Alafog'. **Presteigne** (Pws) means 'household or community of priests'; **Chepstow** (Gt) is 'market place'; **Mounton** (Gt) means 'village belonging to the monks', namely those of Chepstow Priory. **Welshpool** (Pws) is **Y Trallwng** in Welsh, meaning 'The Pool'; a small tributary joins the Severn here.

Prestatyn (Clw) has a Welsh appearance but is from Old English and is of the same derivation as **Preston**, 'priests' village', which occurs frequently in England and Scotland. From *prēosta-tūn*, it has reached its present form because of the Welsh habit of stressing the last syllable but one. **Rhyl** (Clw) is English *hill*, prefixed with *yr*, the Welsh definite article. The name is paradoxical, as the elevation is but slight.

Linguistically, the Isle of Man has less in common with Wales than with Ireland or Scotland, since Manx belongs to the Goidelic group of Celtic languages, whereas Welsh is Brythonic. There are also many names of Norse origin but both **Castletown** and **Peel** reflect medieval English influence. **Peel**, 'fortress' is named from the castle. This name began its life with a less dignified meaning; originally it was merely 'palisade' but it was extended eventually to refer to every kind of fortification.

Bride and **Andreas** are dedication names, in full **Kirkbride** and **Kirkandreas**, respectively 'church of St Brigid' and 'church of St Andrew'. **Maughold Head** is a promontory named after St Machud, the tutelary saint of **Kirk Maughold**. **Baldrine** is from Manx *Balley drine*, 'farm of the blackthorn'; **Ballakillingan** is 'farm of St Fingan's church'; **Ballymeanagh** is 'middle farm'; **Ballabeg** is 'little farm'. **Stroin Vuigh** is 'yellow headland'. **Douglas**, 'black stream', has counterparts elsewhere in the British Isles.

The long-lasting Scandinavian dominion over the island left its mark on the place-names. **Fleshwick Bay**, like **Fleswick Bay** (Cu/Cba), is 'bay of the flat stones'; as the second element is Old Norse *vík*, *Bay* is superfluous. **Jurby** is 'Dyri's homestead' and **Sulby** 'Soli's farm'. **Ramsey** is from an Old Norse stream name, *Ramsá*, 'wild garlic stream'; the first element is found in some names in England, e.g. **Ramsey** (Ess, Hu/C), but the second component is Old English *ēg*, 'island, or dry ground in a fen'. **Laxey** is 'salmon stream'. The **Calf of Man** is a picturesque (Norse) reference to a smaller island beside a larger one; the term also occurs in the Orkneys: **Calf of Eday** and **Calf of Flotta**.

9. Irish place-names

In the modern Irish language the name for the westernmost of the British Isles is **Éire**. The early name was *Eriu*, whose dative case, *Erinn*, gives the poetic 'Erin'. The English name, **Ireland**, is deceptively similar in form to **England**, but whereas the latter is from *Englaland*, 'land of the Angles', the former attempts to give an English dress to the Gaelic name, so that it can only be rendered by 'land of Eire' or 'country called Éire'. Politically, the island is now divided between the Republic of Ireland in the south and Northern Ireland, which is part of the United Kingdom. Northern Ireland is often called **Ulster**, though it comprises only six of the eight counties of the ancient province.

Ulster has a name of mixed descent; Scandinavian *stathr*, 'place', has been added to the Irish tribal name, *Uladh*. Another tribe, the *Mumhan*, is recalled in **Munster**; the third province name with this termination is **Leinster**, 'place of the *laighen*', referring to a broad-pointed spear used by one of its ancient kings.

Many Irish counties use their county town name prefixed by the work *County*, e.g. **County Down**, from **Down**, 'fortress'. Also derived from Irish *dun* are **Dundrum**, 'fort on the long hill', and **Downpatrick**, 'St Patrick's fortress'. **Armagh**, likewise the name of both city and county, means 'Macha's height', commemorating one of three women in Irish legendary history, though it is not certain which one. North of County Down is **Antrim**, 'one holding', containing within its boundaries the provincial capital, **Belfast**, 'ford at the sandbank'. Two places in this county, **Ballymena** and **Ballycastle**, include the frequent Irish element *baile*, 'farm, village, town'; they are 'middle town' and 'town by the castle' respectively. **Ballymoney**, in this and other counties, is 'town by a shrubbery'. **Ballyclare** has a different origin and is 'pass of the plain'; **Clare**, 'plain', occurs elsewhere in Ireland.

Carrickfergus, 'rock of Fergus', shows the characteristic order of elements. **Larne** is from a personal name, Lathair — a legendary character. **County Derry** is named from the town, evidently sited near an 'oak wood'. The extended form **Londonderry** commemorates the association of London merchants with the town from the time of James I. **Coleraine** is 'nook of the ferns'. The name of **Tyrone**, 'land of Owen', celebrates the memory of Owen, the ancestor of the O'Neills, though the territory of this hero, who died in AD 465, was much more extensive than the present-day county. **Clogher**, 'stony place', is found in this county and in Mayo. **Fermanagh** recalls 'the men of Monach', a tribe of Leinstermen who had to leave that province after killing its king, Enna. Another personal name, that of Cethlenn, wife of the great chief Balor, is possibly the second element in **Enniskillen**, 'island of Cethlenn'.

Donegal, in the Irish Republic, is 'fortress of the foreigners'. According to the Annals of Ulster, a Danish fortress was destroyed here in 1159. Elsewhere in Ireland, *Gall*, 'foreigner', often refers to Englishmen. **Galway**, however, does not contain this element but means 'stony place'. **Monaghan** is in Irish **Muineachan**, 'little shrubbery', being the diminutive form of *muine*, found in **Ballymoney** (above) and in **Moniven** in County Galway, which is 'shrubbery of the mead', doubtless alluding to the brewing there of that drink.

Sligeach, the Irish name for **Sligo**, originally that of the river, means 'abounding in shells'. **Collooney**, in the same county, is 'nook of the thicket'; **Tobercurry** contains an element frequently found in Gaelic place-names, *tobar*, 'well'. This County Sligo name means 'well of the cauldron'. In **County Mayo** ('plain of the yews') are found **Ballina**, 'ford mouth', and **Ardnaree**, 'height of the executions', as this was where the Four Maels, the murderers of Guaire Aidhne, king of **Connaught**, were hanged. The names of the province is derived from that of a tribe, the *Connachta*.

In the far west of Ireland is the district of **Connemara**, taking its name from the descendants of Conmac, son of Fergus, ex-king of Ulster, and Maev, queen of Connaught. The *Conmaicne* tribe held several territories; the one by the sea was called *Conmaicne-mara*, 'seaside *Conmaicne*'. Within the boundaries of **County Clare** ('level place') lies much of the great **Lough Derg**, 'lake of the red'. According to legend, the lake was dyed with the blood of Eochy MacLuchta, king of south Connaught, who plucked out his own eye at the request of the poet Aithirne. The river **Shannon** is named after an ancient goddess, as are the several rivers **Boyne**. **Limerick** is a 'barren spot'; **Roscommon** is 'Coman's wood', from the saint who founded a monastery there and died in the seventh century. **Tipperary** is 'well of Ara', alluding to the territory in which the town is situated. **Leitrim** is 'grey ridge'.

Dispite its Saxon appearance, **Longford** is completely Irish and means 'fortified house'. **Mullingar**, in Westmeath, is 'crooked mill'. This county was created in the sixteenth century from part of **Meath**, 'middle', the great territory which in earlier times had formed the fifth province of Ireland. In the far west, on the river Shannon stands **Athlone**, the 'ford of Luan'. **Offaly** is '(territory of) sons of Failghe', i.e. the descendants of Ros of the Rings, eldest of the thirty sons of Cahirmore. **Tullamore** is 'big hill' and **Banagher** 'peaked hill'.

Leix is named after an Ulster chieftain, Lughaidh Laeghseach, who came to the aid of the king of Leinster in the second century AD. In return he received extensive lands, now called by the tribal name, **Laois**, of which **Leix** is the anglicised form. **Abbeyleix** is accordingly self-explanatory. Another famous ecclesiastical centre is nearby — **Durrow**, 'oak plain'. The saint known in Scotland as Kenneth is commemorated in **Kilkenny**, 'cell of Cainnech'. **Freshford** is a bad translation of the Irish *Achadur*, 'fresh field'.

Waterford and **Wexford** are both of Scandinavian origin. The former is 'inlet of the wether' and the latter 'sea-washed inlet'. **Lismore** is 'big fort'; **Tramore**, on the coast is 'big strand'. **Tralee** is 'shore of the river Lee'; **Killarney** is 'church of the sloes'. **Listowel**, **Liscarroll** and **Liscahane** are all fort-names, commemorating respectively Tuathal, Carroll and Cathan. Ciar, the eldest son of Fergus and Maev, gave his name to **Kerry**. **Cork** is derived from *Corcach-nar-mumhan*, 'the great marsh of Munster'. At the edges of this county are two bays: **Bantry**, on the west, and **Youghal**, on the east. The former keeps alive the memory of the *Beanntraighe*, the 'race of Beann', descendants of one of the sons of Conor MacNessa, king of Ulster. **Youghal** is 'yew wood', from an ancient wood on the hill near which the town was built. **Cloyne** is from *Cluain-uamha*, 'meadow of the cave'; **Mallow** is 'plain of the rock'. The Irish spelling of **Cobh** disguises the fact that it is simply the English 'cove'. **Skibbereen** is 'place frequented by boats'; **Kinsale** is 'head of the brine'. **Kildare** is 'church of the oak tree', alluding to an ancient oak, traditionally much loved by St Brigid. The town of **Carlow** derives its name from the 'fourfold lake' said to have been formed there by the river, but of which there is now no trace. **Wicklow** and **Arklow**, however, are Scandinavian formations, meaning respectively 'Viking's meadow' and 'Arnkel's meadow'. **Leixlip**, from Old Norse *Laxhlaup*, 'salmon leap', is named from a cateract on the river Liffey.

On the same river was to be found the 'black pool' which gave the name **Dublin**, though the capital of the Republic is now called in Irish **Baile Atha Cliath**, 'town at the hurdle ford'. **Naas**, said to have been the earliest residence of the kings of Leinster, means 'assembly place'; **Maynooth** is 'plain of Duadhat'. Reference to trees are to be found in **Lucan**, 'place of the elms', and **Trim**, 'elder-tree place', in County Meath, from the trees that grew near a ford across the Boyne. **Trummery**, in County Antrim, has the same meaning. **Drogheda** is 'bridge by a ford'; **Kells** is the much eroded form of *Ceanannus*, 'chief residence'. Laoghaire, who was king of Ireland from 428 to 458, is commemorated in the name **Dun Laoghaire**.

10. Place-names in Scotland

Scotia, in the earliest records, was the name applied to Ireland, because the Scots lived there then. In course of time, however, both the people and the name were transferred to the northern part of Britain. The ancient name, **Caledonia**, now usually explained as '(land of the) battle cry', is incorporated in **Dunkeld** (Tsd), 'fort of the Caledonians' and in the mountain name **Schiehallion** (Tsd), in Gaelic *Sid Chailleann*, 'Caledonians' fairy hill'.

Scotland seems not to have offered such strong resistance as Ireland to foreign influences in her place-names. In addition to three varieties of Celtic names (Pictish, Gaelic and British), Scandinavian and English elements are also found. The **Shetland Islands** have a Norse name, 'hilt land'. In **Orkney**, Scandinavian *ey* was added to the earlier name *Orc*. The *-n-* of this name is possibly a relic of Gaelic *inis*, 'island'. The pre-Celtic first element probably means 'boar' and may allude to a totem.

Another animal name occurs in that of the most northerly county, **Caithness**, 'cape of the Cat (tribe)', referring specifically to North Cape, but now applied to the whole territory as far as **Sutherland**, which the tribe also occupied. Not merely the termination but the entire name here is Norse, as this was the 'south land' of those based in Orkney. **Cape Wrath** (Hld) seems appropriate for a promontory on a wild coast but is Old Norse *hvarf*, 'turning of the land', the origin also of **Quarff**, in Shetland. *Tarvodunum*, 'bull fort', the early Celtic name for **Dunnet Head** (Hld), sheds some light on the meaning of **Thurso** (Hld). Its earliest recorded name, Celtic *Tarvodubron*, 'bull water', became *Thjorsá* in Old Norse translation, but, owing to the frequency of references to the god Thor in place-names, this was adapted to *Thorsá*, 'Thor's river'.

Wick (Hld) is from the frequent Old Norse term for 'bay, inlet of the sea', *vík*, but Old English *wîc* is the source of names in the Lowlands ending in *-wick*, 'outlying farm, dependent estate, dwelling', e.g. **Hawick** (Bdrs), 'farm with a hedge', and **Prestwick** (Scl), 'priest's dwelling'.

Durness (Hld), 'deer promontory', is of Scandinavian origin, as are **Helmsdale, Brora** and **Golspie** (all Hld), respectively 'Hjalmund's valley', 'river with a bridge' and 'Gulli's village'. **Lairg** (Hld), however, is Gaelic, 'thigh'; **Gairloch** (Hld) is 'short loch'. **Dounreay** (Hld) is 'fort on a mound'. **Dornoch** (Hld), also of Gaelic origin, is 'pebbly place', implying that the pebbles were of a size to fill the fist (*dorn*), and therefore of use as weapons. **Nairn** (Hld) is named from its river, the pre-Celtic appellation meaning 'flowing water'. **Tain** (Hld) is also called after its local river, which again has a name of generalised meaning (from a root signifying 'flow, dissolve, melt'). **Dingwall** (Hld) and similar names are discussed in chapter 6. **St Kilda** (WI), in the outermost Hebrides, does not commemorate a saint at all, although much effort has been spent in trying to identify this elusive holy person. Just as in England the name **Sarum** (W) arose from a misreading of the abbreviated form of *Sarisberi*, so the new saint was added to the calendar from a mistaken reading of *Skildar*, 'shields', on early maritime charts.

Inverness (Hld), 'mouth of the Ness', is one of a large group of names beginning with Inver- (Gaelic *Inbhir*), 'river mouth, confluence'. The meaning of the ancient name **Ness** is unknown. Besides river names, as in this instance and in **Inveraray** (Scl), **Inverurie** (Gra) and **Invernairn**, now **Nairn** (Hld), the element is occasionally followed by topographical or other terms, e.g. **Inverquharity** (Tsd), 'confluence of the couple', being the place where two streams together enter the Esk, and **Invernauld** (Hld), 'confluence of cliffs'. **Invergordon** (Hld) dates only from the eighteenth century and commemorates the landowner there, Sir Alexander Gordon. In **Lossiemouth** (Gra) the English word *mouth* is added to a Gaelic river-name meaning 'river of herbs'.

Moray is 'sea settlement'. **Banff** (Gra) means 'pig'; both this and **Elgin** (Gra) are said to be covert or poetic references to Ireland, the ancient homeland of the Highlanders. The Scots from Ireland brought with them their Goidelic language, but the earlier inhabitants used dialects akin to those of the Britons of the south and to modern Welsh. The Celtic name **Keith** (Gra), Brythonic and not Goidelic, means 'wood' and may be compared with names like **Chetwode** (Bk), but the Scottish example lacks the explanatory translation that constitutes the second element in that name. **Dalkeith** (Lo), 'meadow of the wood', has a Gaelic element prefixed. **Peterhead** (Gra), 'St Peter's headland', is one of the rare English names in this part of Scotland.

Aberdeen (Gra) and **Arbroath** (Tsd) both include the Brythonic element *Aber-*, 'river mouth', found so preponderantly in Pictish areas that it is almost certainly from the language of that people. These are 'mouth of Don' and 'mouth of Brothock' respectively. **Aberfeldy** (Tsd), unlike most names of the class, does not include the name of its river (which is the **Moness Burn** — *i mbun eas*, 'near waterfalls') but alludes to Peallaidh, a water demon, and is best rendered 'demon-haunted river mouth'. The hundred or more names commencing with *Pit-*, from **Pitalmit** (Hld) to **Pityoulish** (Hld), have been much discussed. The argument is about such matters as the identity of the Pictish people, whether they were one people or more, what language or languages they spoke, their relations with their neighbours, and so on, and the entire discussion can be said to be crystallised in these names. The first element means 'portion'; **Pitlochry** (Tsd) means 'stony ground portion', with a possible reference to stepping stones. This 'Pictish' first element is almost always combined with a Gaelic specifier, as in this name. **Pitmaduthy** (Hld) means 'Macduff's portion', **Pettymuck** (Gra), 'pig portion', **Pettyvaich** (Tsd), 'share with cow-shed', and **Pittenweem** (Fife), 'share with a cave'. In **Pityoulish** (Hld), the second component means 'bright station', a station being a stance or stopping place where a drover might leave his animals for the night.

Other elements of possibly Pictish origin include *pert*, 'copse, thicket', *pevr*, 'beautiful', and *lanerc*, 'glade, clearing'. The first of these is found in **Perth** (Tsd), formerly known as **St Johnstoun**. There are several rivers in Scotland called **Peffer**; **Strathpeffer** (Hld) is 'valley of the river Peffer'. Of the place-names containing the element *lanerc*, the best known is

Lanark (Scl), and there are two instances of **Lendrick** (Tsd). There were also non-Gaelic Celts in the south of Scotland, i.e. outside the area usually spoken of as Pictland. They left behind such names as **Brechin** (Tsd — from the personal name Brychan), **Peebles** (Bdrs, 'temporary dwellings'), and **Glasgow** (Scl). The last, meaning 'green hollow', shares a second element with *Lithgow*, 'damp hollow', found in **Linlithgow** (Lo, 'lake of Lithgow'). **Dumbarton** (Scl, 'fortress of the Britons'), the chief settlement of the Strathclyde Britons, was called by them *Alclut*, 'rock of Clyde'. The spelling **Dunbartonshire** for the county name is a modern bureaucratic invention which contradicts normal linguistic development.

The first element in **Kirkcaldy** (Fife) is not *kirk*, 'church', but the British word which became *Caer* in Welsh, redundantly prefixed to a word which already meant 'hard fort'. The same first element is found in **Kirkintilloch** (Scl, 'fort at the head of the eminences'). In names like **Kirkbride, Kirkconnel** and **Kirkcudbright** (all D&G), the Scots word *kirk*, 'church', is prefixed to a saint's name — respectively, Brigid, Congal and Cuthbert. The Celtic word order (with defining element following the generic term *kirk*) occurs in these names even though *Kirk*- and (in some of them) the name of the tutelary saint are non-Celtic. This probably came about by the replacement of Gaelic *Cill* by Germanic *Kirk*; the former remains in **Kilbride** (Scl, WI), **Kilmarnock** (Scl), **Kildonan** (Hld, Scl, WI) and **Kilpatrick** (Scl).

Fort William, Fort Augustus and **Fort George** (all Hld) commemorate English military activity in Scotland during the seventeenth and eighteenth centuries. The oldest of these garrisons was founded in 1690 and named in honour of King William III; the second celebrates Prince William Augustus, Duke of Cumberland, and the third King George II. The survival of these names is surprising.

Oban (Scl) means 'little bay'. **Argyll** is 'coastland of the Gael'. **Bute** (Scl) is possibly '(island of) fire', referring to signal fires. **Mull** (Scl) is 'prominent island' — either topographically or by reason of some other importance. *Mull* in such names as **Mull of Kintyre** (Scl) means 'promontory, cape'. **Tobermory** (Scl) means 'well of (St) Mary'. **Motherwell** (Scl) may also be interpreted in this way, but there is considerable doubt about this name. **Ayr** (Scl) takes its name from the river, which has one of the pre-Celtic river names of a type found throughout Britain and in continental Europe. **Airdrie** (Scl) is possibly 'high slope'. **Stirling** (Cen) is obscure, but a river-name may be the origin of the first element.

About the second element of **Edinburgh** (Lo) there is no dispute: it is undoubtedly Old English *burh*, 'fortification, fortified place', but there has been serious disagreement about the first component. One view is that it represents the original (Celtic) name of the place, to which the explanatory -*burh* was added by Angles, the equivalent Celtic *Dun* being prefixed to *Eidin* by Britons and Gaels. But partisans of a different view argue that the evidence of forms like *Eduenesburg* and *Edwinesburg* supports the idea that this was a fortress established or defended by King Edwin. There is further historical evidence against this theory, and Celtic *Eidyn* (the meaning of which is unknown) is the more probable origin.

Of the contracted name **Bo'ness** (Lo), the full form (rarely if ever used) is Borrowstounness, 'point of Borrowstoun, i.e. Beornweard's village'. **Falkirk** (Cen, 'speckled church'), is a translation of the Gaelic name *Eaglais Bhreac*; Middle English *fawe* means 'variegated'. **Duns** (Bdrs) and **Largs** (Scl) are names of Gaelic origin to which English -*s* has been added for the plural; they mean 'hillforts' and 'slopes' respectively. **Lothian**, 'territory of Leudonus', was an ancient province, later divided into **East Lothian** or **Haddington(shire)** ('estate of Hada's kin'), **Edinburgh** or **Mid Lothian**, and **Linlithgow(shire)** or **West Lothian**. After the local government reorganisation of 1974 the three counties have been re-united as Lothian region.

11. Forests, rivers and hills

In Roman times thick forests covered much of the British countryside, and the few settlements within their bounds were in natural or man-made clearings. The survival of so few forest names down to the present day demonstrates the scale of the destruction that has taken place, though the term *forest* was used not only of extensive woodlands but also of large areas, not necessarily heavily wooded, reserved for hunting. The earliest record of **Sherwood Forest** (Nt) is dated 986, when it took the form *Scyryuda*, for *Scyrwuda*, 'county wood', possibly because of its proximity to the boundary. **The Lyme**, 'elmy place', was once a great forest covering parts of Staffordshire, Shropshire, Cheshire and south-east Lancashire (now Greater Manchester). It is referred to in **Burslem** (St, 'Burgheard's (estate in) the Lyme'), **Ashton under Lyne** (La/GM) and **Newcastle under Lyme** (St).

The preposition *under* occurs quite often with forest names, meaning 'in the shelter of' or 'under the jurisdiction of'; besides the two instances just mentioned there are also **Shipton under Wychwood** (Oxf) and **Barton under Needwood** (St). **Shipton** is 'sheep farm' and **Barton** 'barley farm', both implying granges or outlying farms at some distance from a manor or settlement. In

Wychwood the first element is *Hwicce*, the name of a large tribe of the west Midlands. **Needwood** is 'wood resorted to in case of need' — possibly that of avoiding the law. The affix in **Wotton Underwood** (Bk) was formerly *under Bernewode*, alluding to **Bernwood Forest**, 'wood by a burial mound'.

In Northamptonshire **Rockingham Forest** and **Cliffe Forest** take their names from **Rockingham** ('homestead of Hrōc's people') and **King's Cliffe** ('the king's manor at the steep hill'). **Whittlewood Forest** commemorates a man called Witela. **Salcey Forest** is a 'place of willows'; **Selwood Forest** (So) also alludes to willows, but the derivation is from Old English *sealh* rather than. Old French *salceie*. **Wyre Forest** (Wo/H&W) is named after the Wigoran tribe, referred to also in the name **Worcester**.

The New Forest (Ha) has been so called for nearly nine hundred years, having been reserved as a hunting ground for William I. **The Weald** (ESus, Ha, K, WSus) is from Old English *wald*, '(upland) forest'. In **North Weald Bassett** (Ess) this element refers to **Epping Forest**, the usual name of which is from **Epping** (Ess), 'people of the upland'. *Wald* is combined with the personal name Cod in **Cotswolds** (Gl, Oxf). The term later came to mean 'high open ground', as in **The Wolds** of the East Midlands.

Delamere Forest (Ch) is named from a 'mere' or lake, probably Blakemere, near Eddisbury. **Mondrem Forest** (Ch) means 'pleasure ground'. **Ashdown Forest** (ESus) is 'ash tree hill'. The forest of **Galtres** (NRY), 'boar brushwood', was evidently much favoured by those beasts; when hunted, wild boar make for the thickest brushwood they can find.

Allerdale Forest (Cu/Cba) is in the valley of the river Ellen. **Kieder Forest** (Nb) is from the name of a river which, like that of the several rivers **Calder** (Cu/Cba, La, WRY/WYk), originates in a Celtic term for 'violent water'. Other river-names referring to rapidity or strength include **Stour** (Do, Sf-Ess, Wo/WM-Wo/H&W), **Aire** (WRY/NYk-WYk), **Taw** (Dev), **Test** (Ha), and, in Scotland, **Tay** (Tsd). The **Tweed** (Bdrs-Nb) which for part of its course forms a boundary between Scotland and England, is also named from the strength of its current. Many river-names in all parts of Britain mean simply 'water', 'stream' or the like. Among these are **Avon** (frequent), **Esk** (frequent), **Usk** (Pws-Gt), **Wiske** (NRY/NYk), **Exe** (So-Dev), **Axe** (Do-Dev, So), **Dore** (He/H&W), **Wear** (Du-Du/T&W), **Ouse** and **Wey** (Sr, Do). Besides the **Tyne** in Northumberland (now partly in Tyne and Wear) there is another in East Lothian, and a number of river-names have similar or related forms in different parts of Britain. The **Alne**, probably 'flowing one', on which stand **Alnwick, Alnham** and **Alnmouth** (Nb), is related in origin to the **Ellen** in Cumbria and to the **Alness** (Hld) in Scotland, at the mouth of which stands the town of the same name.

Some names describe such obvious characteristics of rivers as colour or sound; others allude to vegetation. There are numerous rivers called **Blackwater, Black Brook** or **Blackburn**, and a number of names of Celtic derivation mean 'black or dark stream', e.g. **Dove** (Db-St, WRY/SYk), **Douglas** (La), **Dawlish Water** (Dev), and the several rivers **Dulas** or **Dulais** in Wales. Often the blackness is not that of the water in the river but of the soil in its bed. One of the tributaries of the **Blackwater** (Ha, Brk) is the **Whitewater**. The **Grindle Brook** (Dev) is named from the dominant colour of its valley, as the alternative **Greendale** confirms. Oak trees, possibly once in extensive woods, are referred to in the names of the several rivers **Derwent**, as well as in **Darwen** (La), **Dart** (Dev) and **Darent** (K). **Leam** (Nth-Wa) and **Leven** (frequent) are from a word meaning 'elm'.

The Anglo-Saxons often used an explanatory term like *burna* or *brōc*, both meaning 'brook', in stream names, many of which were later applied to settlements. Personal names are found in **Cottesbrooke** and **Lilbourne** (Nth). Other streams are described by some quality of the water, e.g. **Saltburn** (NRY/Clev) and **Colburn** (NRY/NYk), the latter being 'cool stream'. Clear water is indicated in **Sherburn** (ERY/NYk), **Shirburn** (Oxf), **Sherborne** (Do, Gl, Ha) and **Shirebrook** (Db), whereas that of **Fulbrook** (Bk, Wa) and **Skidbrooke** (L) was the opposite. **Cranborne** (Do) and **Enborne** (Brk, Ha) refer respectively to the heron and the duck.

Old English *ēa*, 'river', which has become **Eye** (Lei) and **Yeo** (Dev, Do-So, So/Av), occurs as a final element in **Waveney** (Sf-Nf), 'fen river', and **Mersey** (Ch/GM-La/Mer), 'boundary river', so called because it separated the Anglo Saxon kingdoms of Northumbria and Mercia. In **Tachbrook** (Wa, Wo) the first element, meaning 'marker, indicator', also refers to a boundary. The importance of streams as boundaries is also indicated by such names as **Marlbrook** (Sa) and **Meersbrook** (Db, WRY/SYk). **Tyburn** (Mx/GL) has a similar meaning, though the first element is a different one; this stream was in 959 the boundary of Westminster Abbey's estates. The name was changed to *Marybourn*, into which -*le*- unwarrantably intruded, to make the place-name **Marylebone** (still pronounced with three syllables rather than four).

Loudwater (Bk) bears the former designation of the stream on which it stands, now the **Wye**. The later name, a 'back-formation' from **Wycombe** (Bk), was first applied to the river by military cadets engaged in surveying exercises. The process of back-formation, in which a town name is adapted to form that of a river, can be seen also in **Cam**, from **Cambridge** ('bridge over the Granta, i.e. shallow or muddy river'), and in **Chelmer**, from

Chelmsford (Ess — 'Cēolmǣr's ford'). From **Romford** (Ess/GL) and **Widford** Ess), both meaning 'wide ford', come the river names **Rom** and **Wid**. **Chelt** is a back-formation from **Cheltenham** (Gl), 'riverside pasture by *Celte*, i.e. hill'. **Hiz** is almost certainly from **Hitchin** (Hrt — a tribal name, '(place) among the Hicce').

The **Severn**, probably meaning 'milky', was mentioned in the *Annals* of Tacitus. **Trent** and **Tarrant** (Do) are from British *Trisantona*, 'traveller, trespasser', alluding to liability to floods or to the tidal phenomenon known as the 'eagre'. The estuary of the Ouse and Trent is called the **Humber**, a name borne by a number of smaller streams elsewhere in England. The meaning is obscure, but it may be 'good river' or a similar complimentary name, intended to placate the dark forces of a dangerous stretch of water.

The names of the several English rivers **Don**, such as that on which **Doncaster** (WRY/SYk) stands, are not related to the Scottish **Don** (Gra) and **Doon** (Scl). The former group are from an element, found also in Danube, meaning 'river', whereas the Scottish names are from early Celtic *Devona*, a river goddess. **Dee**, however, in Scotland, Wales and England is derived from *Deuā*, 'goddess, holy one'. **Thames**, perhaps 'flowing one', was not surprisingly recorded very early; Caesar refers to it as *Tamesis*, and Ptolemy (*c*. AD 150) as *Tamesa*. To this name are probably related **Tamar** (Co-Dev), **Tame** (frequent), **Thame** (Bk-Oxf) and (in Scotland) **Tain** (Hld) and **Tay** (Tsd).

A number of hill names in England are of Celtic origin. **Malvern** (Wo/H&W) means 'bare hill'; **Bredon**, in the same county, is derived from British *brigā*, 'hill', with an English suffix, also meaning 'hill', added. **Pendle Hill** (La) is interesting as a 'triplicated' form; to the Celtic word *penno*, 'summit', was added Old English *hyll*, which merged to form **Pendle**; when the significance of both elements was no longer understood, *Hill* was added. **Pennine** is apparently related to British *penno* but early documentation is lacking. Another British word for 'mountain' is found in **Mynde** (He/H&W) and **Longmynd** (Sa); it also occurs in **Mendip** (So), the second element of which is obscure. The **Chiltern** Hills also bear a Celtic name meaning 'high places'. The name of the **Quantock** Hills (So) is derived from a British word meaning 'circle, rim'. **Helvellyn** (Cu/Cba) has a Celtic appearance but it was first recorded only in the sixteenth century and its origin has not been determined.

The highest mountain in Wales is commonly known by its English name, current for nine hundred years, of **Snowdon** (Gd), 'snow hill'; its Welsh designation, **Yr Wyddfa**, means 'cairn place'. **Pumlumon** (Dyf), 'five (beacon) lights' (**Plynlimon** is the anglicised version), records the importance of mountain tops in

Primitive Welsh *cadeir* is found also in **Caterham** (Sr, 'village by hill called *Cater*') and in **Chadderton** (La/GM), **Catterton** (WRY/NYk) and **Chatterley** (St).

In Scotland, the **Trossachs** (Cen) are the 'transverse hills'. The meaning of **Grampians** is not known, but their former name **The Mounth** signifies simply 'the mountain'. **Cairngorm** (Gr-Hld) means 'blue heap of rock'. **Benbrack**, 'speckled hill', is the name of several Irish and Scottish mountains. **Benbeg**, in County Galway, means 'little hill'; **Ben More**, 'big hill', occurs frequently. **Ben Nevis** (Hld) takes its name from the river **Nevis**, 'the spiteful one'.

Among the Norse elements in mountain names are *skuti*, 'overhanging rock', and *fell (fjall)*, 'rough hill'. The former occurs in **Scout Crag** (We/Cba) and possibly in **Skiddaw** (Cu/Cba), 'craggy hill'. The first part of **Kinder Scout** (Db) is Celtic and means 'high hill'. Old Norse *fjall* is found in **Snaefell** (IOM), 'snow hill', occasionally in Scotland, e.g. **Goat Fell** on Arran (Scl), and frequently in the English Lake District. In **Sca Fell** (Cu/Cba), the Scandinavian element is added to an original Celtic name, meaning 'bald hill'. Tree names are found with *fell* e.g. **Ash Fell** and **Bire Fell** (We/Cba). **Whinfell** (Cu/Cba) is 'hill overgrown with furze'.

12. Boundary changes and place-names

Although many old names were utilised for areas brought into being by the local government reorganisation of 1974, some areas had names imposed upon them to which objections were raised. The councils of Greater London and the metropolitan counties have been abolished but the names have been retained for these areas. Within twenty years, however, further changes were proposed. At the time of writing, the suggested modifications have not been implemented, and so details in this book have been left unaltered. The latest reorganisation is unlikely to produce a crop of new names. Indeed, it seems probable that a number of places will revert to earlier designations.

Middlesex had already disappeared with the creation of **Greater London** some years before. In the major reorganisation **Westmorland**, **Rutland** and **Huntingdon and Peterborough** were also removed from the list of English counties. Some of those remaining, often with considerably modified boundaries, retained their former names. **Hereford and Worcester** became the title of the combination of those two shires, and **Cumbria** for the Lake District area comprising Cumberland, Westmorland and part of Lancashire. Further changes took place quite quickly after reorganisation, as a result of public reactions; the adoption, for instance, of the traditional contraction **Salop** as the official title of the shire was soon cancelled and the reorganised county is now **Shropshire** once again. Some new counties utilised existing names of places or rivers, including **Avon** (from the river often known as the Bristol Avon), **Tyne and Wear** and **Cleveland** ('hilly district'). Other new areas adopted as names terms which had previously been used, rather vaguely, for geographic regions, such as **West Midlands**, **Merseyside** and **Greater Manchester**.

The boundaries of Yorkshire were redrawn. The East Riding became part of the new county of **Humberside**; two 'metropolitan counties' were set up in populous industrial areas — **West Yorkshire** and **South Yorkshire** — and the remainder (apart from a segment contributed to Cleveland) is now **North Yorkshire**.

Some of the districts into which Northern Ireland is now divided use former county names, e.g. **Armagh**, 'height of Macha', **Antrim** and **Down**. Others bear the names of towns, such as **Belfast, Strabane**, 'white riverside land', and **Omagh**, '—— plain', the meaning of the first element being unknown. **Castlereagh** means 'grey castle' and **Dungannon** 'Geanman's fort'. **Lisburn**, the meaning of which is uncertain, was formerly *Lisnagarvey*, 'fort of the gamesters'. **Limavady** is 'fort of the dog'; **Banbridge** is 'bridge over the river Bann, i.e. goddess'.

A few of the names of Scottish regions, e.g. **Borders, Central** and **Highland**, are self-explanatory, at least with the help of a map of the country. Old county names are retained in **Fife** (said to commemorate Fib, one of the seven sons of Cruithne, the founder of the Picts), and **Dumfries and Galloway**, the former in this pair being 'fort or hillock of the copse' and the latter 'among the foreign Gaels', alluding to invaders from the west. **Tayside** (from the river name) comprises Perthshire and Angus; **Strath-clyde** ('valley of the Clyde') embraces a large area on the west coast and its hinterland. The names of large towns and of the old counties have been used for some of the districts, secondary administrative areas within the new regions. Those of Central region, for instance, are **Falkirk** ('mottled church'), **Stirling** and **Clackmannan**, the last being 'stone of Manu'.

Districts in Highland region include **Ross and Cromarty**, **Caithness**, **Nairn** and **Sutherland**. Elsewhere, names of river valleys abound, e.g. **Annandale and Eskdale** in Dumfries and Galloway region; **Tweeddale** and **Ettrick and Lauderdale** in Borders region; and **Cumnock and Doon Valley**, **Inverclyde** and **Clydebank** in Strathclyde region. The frequent occurrence of combinations joined by 'and' was doubless brought about through pressure of local sensitivity, but it does not aid clarity in such lists as these.

New Welsh county names have been explained in chapter 8. District names have again been found from those of some former counties, e.g. **Carmarthen** and **Ceredigion** (Cardigan) in Dyfed, and **Ynys Môn** (Anglesey), **Arfon** (Caernarvonshire) and **Meirionnydd** in Gwynedd. Names of rivers and their valleys appear frequently: **Cynon Valley**, **Rhymni Valley** and **Ogwr** ('dagger (-like river)'), are districts in Mid Glamorgan; **Alyn and Deeside** is a district in Clwyd.

Names of former counties also occur as district names in England, e.g. **Huntingdon** in Cambridgeshire and **Rutland** in Leicestershire; those of cities and large towns are understandably utilised within the metropolitan counties: **Bradford**, **Leeds** and **Wakefield** in West Yorkshire and **Birmingham, Coventry** and **Wolverhampton** in West Midlands. Most districts in the new county of Humberside are called by the names of towns formerly in the East Riding of Yorkshire or the Parts of Lindsey in Lincolnshire, e.g. **Scunthorpe** ('Skuma's dependent settlement'), **Grimsby, Beverley** ('beaver stream') and **Kingston upon Hull**.

Some districts have been given the names of ancient hundreds or wapentakes, the former administrative subdivisions of counties before a more sophisticated system was introduced in the nineteenth century. Probably the best known use of the term *hundred* is in the **Chiltern Hundreds**, the stewardship of which disqualifies a person from further service as a member of Parliament. There are five Chiltern Hundreds in Oxfordshire (Binfield, Ewelme, Langtree, Lewknor and Purton), but it is to the three in Buckinghamshire (Stoke, Desborough and Burnham) that the royal stewardship applies. The Buckinghamshire district of **Chiltern** is not exactly coterminous with the ancient group of hundreds. **Dacorum** district in Hertfordshire uses a name meaning 'Danish (hundred)'. The hundred of **Tendring** in Essex, of uncertain meaning, provides one district name in that county, a second being **Rochford**, 'ford of the hunting dog'. **Spelthorne** district in the present county of Surrey also bears a hundred name, meaning 'speech thorn-tree'; but this was a hundred of Middlesex and was a fragment transferred from that county to Surrey when Greater London was created. Nottinghamshire district names include those of the wapentakes of **Broxtowe** ('Brōcwulf's place') and **Bassetlaw** ('mound of the *Bærnedsǣte*'), the second element being an eroded form of the name of an ancient Mercian tribe. **Rushcliffe**, 'brushwood-covered hill', is the third of these districts; this was a wapentake whose meeting place was at Court Hill in **Gotham** (Nt, 'goat village'). **Ryedale** wapentake (NRY) has supplied the name for a district in North Yorkshire; like **Rievaulx**, in the same area, this name signifies 'valley of the river Rye', the British river-name meaning 'stream'. **Richmondshire**, also in North Yorkshire, revives the name of the Honour of Richmond, which combines two early wapentakes of the North Riding. The **Langbaurgh** district of the new county of Cleveland looks back to the names of two North Riding wapentakes (East and West Langbargh), which were in turn derived from the name of a high, narrow ridge called **Langbaurgh**, 'long hill', in Great Ayton.

Some districts in Lincolnshire utilise the names of the former Parts, e.g. **North** and **South Kesteven**, **South Holland** and **East** and **West Lindsey**. Names of natural regions used in other counties include **Broadland** in Norfolk (the **Norfolk Broads**, former peat beds now flooded and used as waterways) and **Fenland** in Cambridgeshire.

Similarity of district names may cause confusion. **Wansbeck** in Northumberland, for instance, from a river-name of unknown meaning, is not unlike **Wansdyke** in Avon, from 'Woden's dyke', an ancient British earthwork built to resist Saxon invaders. **Sedgefield** ('Cedd's open country') is in County Durham, but **Sedgemoor** is in Somerset. The districts of **Wear Valley**, in County Durham, and **Tynedale**, in Northumberland, bear names that might seem more appropriate within the boundaries of their neighbour, the new county of Tyne and Wear.

13. Field-names, street-names and scope for practical work

In addition to natural features, regions, counties, towns and villages, there are countless other places whose names can be profitably studied. Written records of street names, apart from nameplates in the thoroughfares themselves, are restricted to large-scale plans, directories and town guides. Fields are not often marked with their names, which can be found only in sale particulars, 'terriers', estate maps, rent books and similar documents.

A study of the parish tithe map or of the sale particulars of farm land will reveal such names as **Eleven Acres, Bull Piece, Duffers Close, Priestholme, Oakshot, Barber's Mead** and **Upper Carr Field**. Acreage names are very common. In the form **Eleven Acres** or **Eleven Acre Close** the areas are usually accurate: but names like **Seven Acre Meadow** or **Seven Acre Plantation** often bear no relation to actual extent, but refer to land (of any area) adjoining an arable field called **Seven Acres**. In many parts of

Britain **Hundred Acres** (but **Forty Acres** in Leicestershire) designates a very small plot, often of less than half an acre. Small fields may also be called **Handkerchief, Mouse Hall, Wren's Nest** and **Seldom Seen**. Remote fields may be called **World's End, America Close, Canada** or **Botany Bay** or receive such literal names as **Distant Piece, Far Field** or **Furthest Close**.

Shape names range from the approximately accurate, such as **Square Close, The Oval, Round Piece, Triangular Field** or **Many Corners**, to the more imaginative **Harp, Hour Glass, Diamond Piece, Half Moon Close, Spectacles, Elbow, Cocked Hat, Man's Leg** or **Shoulder of Mutton**. Similarity to letters of the alphabet is observed in **Tee Piece, Ell Close, Letter L Field** and (less transparently) **The Yes**.

Some field-names describe the type and quality of soil, e.g. **Sandy Acre, Rocky Piece, Many Stones, Clay Field** and **Bog Furlong**. Figurative names are also common: **Pudding Close, Featherbed** and **Treacle Nook** are used of soft or sticky land; **Leather Close** may indicate very hard soil. **Catsbrain** alludes to a mixture of rough clay and pebbles; **Checker Close, Chess Board** and **Chintz Pattern** are typical names for fields with variegated soil. Other fanciful, ironic or humorous names, e.g. **Pickpocket, Dear Bought, Starvation Hill, Hunger Hill, Carry Nothing, No Gains** and **Greedy Guts**, are frequently applied to impoverished land. Practices to improve the fertility or texture of the soil are recorded in **Marl Piece, Limed Close, Dung Croft** and **Bone Dust Bit**.

The treatment of fallow or grassland by paring and burning is alluded to in **Burn Bake, Burnbacked Meadow, Beaten Flat** and **Push Ploughed Field**; the last name refers to the push-plough or breast plough used for this operation, sometimes known as 'Devonshiring', hence **Devonshire Field** and **Densher Meadow**.

There are frequent references to farm animals. Names like **Bull Piece** or **Bull Pingle** remind us that the bull would be kept apart, sometimes on a very small piece of land. **Calves' Close, Cow Pasture** and **Horsecroft** are common, and to this class belong also **Sheep Close, Eweleaze, Tup Croft** and **Lambleys**. In **Hog Common, Goose Leaze, Chickens Croft, Dog Kennel Close** and **Duck Mead** other farm creatures receive attention. Rabbits and pigeons are not ignored; **Cunny Close, Warren Heath** and **Coney Gree** are evidence of the former; **Dovecote Garth, Culver Close** and **Pigeoncote Croft** indicate an adjacent dovehouse or dovecote, often called *Duffers* or *Ducket* in field names.

Arable crops are named in **Wheat Close, Rye Hill, Barley Croft** and **Oat Furlong**. Less obvious in meaning are **Rylance**, 'rye lands'; **Bear Croft, Barcroft**, 'plot on which hard barley was grown'; **Pilot Field, Pillow Croft**, 'land on which pilled oats were cultivated'; and **Ruworth**, 'rye enclosure'. **Pease Field** and **Peasey**

Close are clear enough, but **Bancroft, Banlands** or **Ballance** less so; these were fields on which beans were grown. **Flaxlands, Lincroft** and **Liquorice Close** point to less familiar crops; woad was grown on **Wadlands**. **Hemp Plot** recalls the cultivation of *Cannabis sativa* for its fibre, from Anglo-Saxon times and even earlier. Potatoes, cabbages, carrots and turnips are all mentioned in field-names, and so are a variety of fodder crops. One instance of **Lucern Field** can be traced back to 1448. **French Grass Field** refers to sainfoin, but more frequent allusions to it include **Sanfoin Field, Sarnfoin Close, Saint Foyne Piece** or even **Sangfoil Field**, in which it seems to be confused with cinquefoil.

The permanence of trees gave them some value as landmarks. **Oak Furlong, Ash Tree Close, Oak and Elm Piece, Crabtree Nooking** and **Sallow Close** provide evidence of woodland, though the land may by now have been completely cleared or entirely built over. **Bark Close, Withy Beds, Sawpit Ground, Coppice Close, Pollard Acre** and **Rail Close** remind us of the details of woodland management and the various uses to which the tree products might be put, including tanning (using oak bark) and basketry. Names can also be found alluding to scabious, poppies, goose-grass (or 'cleavers') and other wild plants.

Besides **Chapel Close, Church Piece** and **Hermitage Meadow**, other ecclesiastical references are found among field-names. Endowed land, the rent from which was applied to particular uses, may be named **Bellrope Piece, The Vestry Light, Lamplands, Candle Close** or **Chalice Field**. **Charity Close** or **Poor's Piece** are frequently found to be owned by the overseers of the poor of the parish. Medieval hospitals may have been supported by **Hospital Croft** or **Spital Close**, and the frequent occurrence of **Chantry Piece** indicates the number of such foundations. **Glebe Piece, Priestholme, Parson's Acre, Vicar's Close** and **Priest Meadows** would have been land worked by, or for the benefit of, the local parson. Other names of this type include **Canonhams, Abbot's Pleck, The Prebend, Sub-Chanter's Dole** and **Monk Croft**.

Reeve Close, Constable's Balk and **Headborough Piece** were assigned to parish officers. **Grammarian's Field** was the perquisite of the schoolmaster and **Hangman's Balk** was probably land cultivated by that official, rather than used for his professional duties. **Hanger**, in place-names and field names, refers to sloping land and not to sites of executions, to which **Gallows Close** or **Gibbet Piece** more probably refer, especially beside a road near the parish border.

Names like **Boundary Piece** or **Bound Close** leave no doubt about the location of the fields, but ownership of such land may be a matter of dispute, signified by **Threaplands** or **No Man's Land**, found in various parts of Britain. Other terms for 'boundary' occur in **Rain Close**, **Mearlands** and **Mark Field**. The 'beating of bounds' at Rogationtide gave rise to **Gospel Piece, Gospel Oak Close, Procession Mere, The Psalms, Paternoster Close, Epistle Field** and **Amen Corner**. **Intak(e)** is a term used for land enclosed from the parish wasteland, and **Assart**, found also as **Sart**, for woodland cleared and brought into cultivation; both occur in field-names.

Surnames often occur. **Cockram's Cowleaze, Cox's Seven Acres, Ramstone's Lot, Congreve's Close** and **Seymour's Meadow** are some of the names of the 'ownership' type occurring in a single Dorset parish. Just as other field-names throw light on agrarian practices of the place in past centuries, those including surnames provide evidence of the occupation of land in the parish by the families concerned.

Oakshot, though applied to enclosed land, refers back to strip cultivation in the open fields. Under that system the great fields, perhaps called **North**, **South** and **East Fields**, or **Church**, **Mill** and **Greenbank Fields**, were divided into groups of strips or holdings; these divisions of the common fields, known as furlongs or shots, were given individual names, such as **Rye Furlong**, **Stoneshot** or **Wheathill**. Like those of modern enclosed fields, these often described the land or its use, But some names appear to have been given arbitrarily. On the enclosure of a parish, land was allocated in single holdings in place of many separate strips distributed through the great fields of a parish, which often numbered more than the three usually described in text books. By consolidation a tenant might receive a whole furlong as his allotment; this could retain its original name, e.g. **Clay Furlong** or **Gravelpit Shot**, or receive an adapted one, such as **Gallows Furlong Close**, or be completely renamed as (for instance) **Barley Close, Third Field** or **Thompson's Piece**. Sometimes division of an entire field led to names like **Upper, Middle** and **Lower Carr Field** for the three parts of **Carr Field**, the name referring to swamp overgrown with brushwood.

Many local historians have found it useful to trace the parish field-names from oral information and from documents in the care of the local church or in the county record office. With precisely recorded evidence from such an investigation, aided by sound local knowledge, it is possible to determine and map the layout of the fields four (or more) centuries ago.

Urban development has concealed much fertile soil beneath domestic and industrial buildings, but names that were once applied to pieces of land now occasionally signify roads or streets. **Long Acre, Tenter Ground**, **Butfield Close**, **The Ham** and **Shortlands** are former field-names in the London area now used as street-names. **Meadowcroft, Glebelands, Lammas Close** and **Greenacres** are applied elsewhere to streets replacing fields that formerly bore these names, though they are sometimes used on new housing estates to attract potential purchasers rather than to pay homage to the past.

The collection and study of the names of streets and roads in a particular area is a realistic project for local historians. The use of various records (old newspapers, early directories, council minutes, etc), normally available in the district, will enable researchers to trace the origin of many street-names. It should be possible to establish, for instance, whether **King Street** commemorates a particular monarch or honours a former citizen with that surname. A neglected class of street-names, mainly found in larger towns, consists of those commemorating builders and developers or their families, sometimes using only Christian names. **Ethel Road, Johnson Terrace** or **Geraldine Place** may be found to be references to otherwise unnoticed local craftsmen and their relatives, records of whom may exist in minute books, building contracts and deeds of sale; details may be discovered from registers of births, deaths and marriages, and a genealogical dimension can be added to the historical interest of such names.

The earliest street-names in a town are likely to be those in its historical centre, but later developments may sometimes cause a **Market Place** or a **High Street** ('principal street') to be located elsewhere than in the chief part of a modern town. **Fore Street** is the name often given to the thoroughfare in front of the gates of an old town. In names like **Northgate** and **Churchgate** the street-names sometimes allude to gates in the town walls but in the Danelaw the termination *-gate* is equivalent to 'road' or 'street'. References to crafts and trades frequently occur in street-names of some antiquity, and groups like **Drapery, Woolmongers' Row** and **Sheep Street** will alert the researcher to the possibility of a history of clothmaking in the town. Obsolete craft names may survive in the street nomenclature, and it may be possible to trace where the cordwainers (leatherworkers), arrowsmiths, lorimers (bitmakers), fletchers and spurriers carried on their trades. Names such as **Chapel Street, Castle Street, Bridge Road, Spa Street** and **Great Central Street** may be valuable clues to buildings or railways no longer in existence. **Steelworks Road, Mill Street** and **Factory Lane** may be highly informative to the industrial archaeologist.

There will be references to national history in such names as **Queen's Road, Jubilee Street, Inkerman Terrace** and **Albert Drive**, to be found in towns both large and small. The references (once identified) may indicate that the streets were built or renamed to commemorate battles or more peaceful celebrations. **Kabul Road, Varna Street, Menin Avenue** or **Omdurman Road** may allude to a development when those places were in the news or an interest on the part of the builder, who may perhaps have performed military service in those places. Sometimes such names are transferred from places abroad where a local landowner also has property.

The interest of street-names is not exclusively historical. In many places groups of streets have names of the same type. Trees, mountain ranges, rivers, flowers, inventors, politicians, poets and painters are all celebrated in this way. It may be the realm of the sociologist or psychologist to explore the motivation for choosing such names, but it is useful to transcribe whatever information local records contain about the process of giving the names to the streets concerned.

The techniques employed in interpreting field-names and street-names are those used in general place-name investigation. For definite or probable explanations, early forms of existing names must be studied within as complete a framework as possible of information about the place at relevant periods, bearing in mind also the linguistic aspects of the names. If all appropriate details are recorded (not forgetting the date, description and location of the documents), an enthusiast with adequate reference material can make valuable contributions to this body of knowledge. Possibly with the aid of others, a local researcher may turn a small project into a published article or booklet; but even short of this, the interested enquirer will soon find many rewards obtainable from discovering place-names.

14. Glossary of technical terms

ADDITION OR AFFIX

An expression attached to a place-name, usually as a separate word or phrase, serving to particularise places bearing such common designations as **Stoke, Sutton, Norton, Newton, Stratford** or **Buckland** ('book land, land held by charter'). Additions may be descriptive, as in **Stony Stratford** (Bk), **Long Newton** (Du/Clev) or **Stoke Dry** (R/Lei); referential, as in **Severn Stoke** (Wo/H&W) or **Sutton by Middlewich** (Ch); manorial, as in **Newton Harcourt** (Lei), **Norton Fitzwarren** (So) or **Bishop's Sutton** (Ha); dedicatory, as in **Chalfont St Giles** (Bk) ('Ceadel's spring, with church dedicated to St Giles'), **Buckland St Mary** (So) or **Stratford St Andrew** (Sf); or a district name, as in **Stokenham** (Dev, in the **South Hams**), **Sutton in Ashfield** (Nt) or **Newton in Makerfield** (La/GM).

BACK-FORMATION

A river name formed from part of a settlement name, irrespective of the meaning of the part so used. In **Alvechurch**

GLOSSARY

(Wo/H&W), **Ogbourne** (W), **Wandsworth** (Sr/GL) and **Chelmsford** (Ess) the first elements are significant parts of the personal names Aelfgyth, Occa, Wendel and Ceolmær; but **Alve**, **Og**, **Wandle** and **Chelmer** have been devised for the rivers, as though the settlement names were derived from them.

COMPOUND

A place-name consisting of two elements (q.v.), e.g. **Dumfries** (D&G), 'fort of the copse' (Gaelic *dún*, *preas*), **Stonehenge** (W), 'gallows made of stone' (OE *stān*, *hengen*), or **Finchampstead** (Brk), 'homestead frequented by finches' (OE *finca*, *hām-stede*).

ELEMENT

One of the units composing a place-name. An element may be a common noun, e.g. Old English *swîn*, 'pig', *slîm*, 'mud', or *stān*, 'stone', any of which may combine with Old English *ford*, as in **Swinford** (Brk/Oxf), **Slimeford** (Co), **Stanford** (Brk, Ess) or **Stamford** (L); or it may be an adjective, e.g. Old English *brād*, 'broad', *rūh*, 'rough', or *walt*, 'unsteady', as in **Bradford** (WRY/WYk), **Rufford** (La) and **Walford** (Do). Personal names may also be elements as in **Aylesbury** (Bk), 'Ægel's fortified place', **Brumby** (L/Hum), 'Brūni's village', **Wokefield** (Brk), 'Wocc's open land', **East Garston** (Brk), 'Esgar's estate', or **Bloxham** (Oxf), 'Blocc's village'.

FOLK-NAME

A place-name consisting simply of the name of the tribe or similar group, e.g. **Woking** (Sr, 'followers of Wocc(a)'), **Epping** (Ess, 'people of the upland'), **Barking** (Ess/GL, 'Berica's people'), and **Ripon** (WRY/NYk, 'among the Hrype tribe').

HABITATION NAME

A place-name denoting a human settlement as distinct from a tribe or a natural feature. In **Repton** (Db, 'farm of the Hrype tribe'), **Brafferton** (Du, 'estate at Bradford or broad ford'), **Wokingham** (Brk, 'village of Wocc's followers'), and **Uppingham** (R/Lei, 'village of the upland people'), the elements *tūn* and *hām* expressly allude to habitations.

HYBRID

A place-name containing elements from two languages, e.g. **Lincoln** (British/Latin), **Makerfield** (La/GM — British/OE: 'open land by a ruin'), **Chatham** (K — British/OE: 'wood homestead'), **Durham** (ON/OE), **Haltwhistle** (Nb — OF/OE: 'high river-fork'), **Rhyl** (Clw — Welsh/English), **Moray** (Gaelic/British), **Largs** (Scl — Gaelic/English). Sometimes a Scandinavian termination replaced an original Old English ending, as in

Holbeck (Nt, 'hollow brook'), the earliest form of which has Old English *brōc*, instead of Old Norse *bekkr*. A Scandinavian personal name is often prefixed to an Old English element, as in **Gamston** (Nt), **Kettlebaston** (Sf) or **Somerleyton** (Sf), in which Old Norse Gamil, Ketil and Sumorlithi are combined with Old English *tūn*. These are known as 'Grimston hybrids', from the frequency of that name in England.

INVERSION COMPOUND

An English place-name in which a personal name (or other word alluding to a person) follows a place-name element, e.g. **Brigsteer** (We/Cba), 'Styr's bridge', **Rigmaden** (We/Cba), 'maiden's ridge'. For Celtic compounds this is the normal order, and so as a technical term for a relatively few names *inversion compound* is going out of use.

MANORIAL AFFIX

An addition indicating a former feudal tenant or lord of the manor. The affix is often a surname, as in **Weston Beggard** (He/H&W), **Wootton Fitzpaine** (Do), **Woodham Ferrers** (Ess), **Weston Favell** (Nth), **Aston Tirrold** (Brk/Oxf), **Newton Blossomville** (Bk) or **Walton Cardiff** (Gl). Sometimes it refers to a profession or office or to the Crown, as in **Monks Risborough** and **Princes Risborough** (Bk), 'brushwood-covered hill', held formerly by the monks of Christchurch, Canterbury, and the Black Prince, respectively. The addition in **Farnham Royal** (Bk) alludes to a manorial duty of supporting the king's right arm at his coronation.

NATURE NAME

A name denoting a natural feature, without reference to a habitation, e.g. **Iscoed** (Clw), 'below the wood', **Trawsfynydd** (Gd), 'across the mountain', **Liverpool** (Mer), 'pool with thick water', **Brewood** (St), 'wood on a hill', **Iver** (Bk), 'steep slope', **Clee** (L/Hum), 'clay', **Tring** (Hrt), 'wooded slope', **Willian** (Hrt) and **Welwyn** (Hrt), '(at) the willow trees'.

POPULAR ETYMOLOGY

The explanation of a place-name by the 'common sense' method of interpreting the present form, or by some association of the components of the modern name, e.g. by taking **Oxshott** (Sr — 'Ocga's allotment of land') to be 'place where an ox was shot', or relating **Barking** (Ess/GL) to the **Isle of Dogs** (Mx/GL), not far away. The process may bring about the replacement of an alien, unpronounceable or unintelligible name by something more familiar, as by substituting **Cutbrawn** and **Palestine** for the Cornish *Coit-bran* ('crow wood') and *Pen-lestyn* ('hill of the fruiting oaks'). Popular etymology in former periods accounts for the development of **York** (see chapter 2) and of **Bishop Auckland** (Du), which began as the transferred former name of Dumbarton (Scl), *Alclut* ('rock on the Clyde'), and was then changed by successive settlers to *Auclent* and *Aucland*, as though derived from Old Norse *klint* ('cliff') and Old English or Old Norse *land*.

REPLACEMENT NAME

A new name (not a contraction or other linguistic development) substituted for an existing designation, e.g. **Dumbarton** (Scl) (in the previous paragraph). **St Albans** (Hrt), **Derby** and **Peterborough** (Nth/C) replaced *Wæclingaceaster*, *Northworthy* and *Medeshamstede*. Some replacements were transferred names: **Richmond** (Sr/GL) was transferred from **Richmond** (NRY/NYk), but the latter (transferred from France) was itself a replacement of an earlier name, *Hindrelac*, 'hind's glade or wood'. Many extant names may be replacements of ancient ones which were never recorded in writing.

SIMPLEX

A place-name composed of a single element, e.g. **Barnes** (Sr/GL), 'barns', **Bootle** (La/Mer), 'dwelling', **Ford** (He/H&W, Sa, So, WSus) and **Stone** (St), consisting respectively of Old English *bere-ærn*, *bothl*, *ford* and *stān*. Other examples are **Paisley** (Scl), 'church' (Gaelic *baslec*), **Cobh** (Cork), 'cove' (Modern English *cove*), and **Peel** (IOM), 'castle' (ME *pele*).

THEME

An ultimate significant component of personal names, place-name elements, etc.

TOPONYMY

The study of place-names. *Onomastics* is the term applied to the study of names in general. In technical works, place-names are often referred to as *toponyms*.

TRANSFERRED NAME

A transplanted place-name, e.g. **Waterloo** (in London and other places), transferred from the site of the battle near Brussels in 1815. In Edinburgh, **Sciennes** is derived from the dedication of a medieval convent to St Catherine of Siena. **Baldock**(Hrt) was named, by returning Crusaders, after **Baghdad** (ME *Baldac*). The monastery at **Bangor** (County Down) was founded by monks from **Bangor** in Gwynedd. Many examples are less than two centuries old, including Welsh hamlets and villages bearing biblical names like **Carmel** (Clw, Dyf, Gd) and **Nebo** (Dyf, Gd) and numerous locations all over Britain called by such names as **Mesopotamia**, **Egypt**, **Dunkirk** and **California**.

15. Books and organisations

FURTHER READING

K. Cameron: *English Place-names* is the best general introduction. **P. H. Reaney**: *The Origin of English Place-names* contains detailed explanations of great interest. **Margaret Gelling**: *Signposts to the Past* and *Place-names in the Landscape* relate English place-name studies to archaeology, history and topography and utilise the results of recent research. **E. Ekwall**: *The Concise Oxford Dictionary of English Place-names* was an important pioneering work and remains a valuable source of information. It has now been joined (and supplemented) by **A. D. Mills**: *A Dictionary of English Place-names*. **O. J. Padel**: *A Popular Dictionary of Cornish Place-names* is a concise glossary of the distinctive names of that county and the Scilly Isles. Works on London names include **J. Field**: *Place-names of Greater London* and **G. Bebbington**: *Street Names of London*. **J. Wittich**: *Discovering London Street Names* is a convenient pocket guide.

For names outside England see **W. F. Nicolaisen**: *Scottish Place-names*, **W. J. Watson**: *The History of the Celtic Place-names of Scotland*, **P. W. Joyce**: *Irish Names of Places*, **B. G. Charles**: *Non-Celtic Place-names of Wales* and *Celtic Place-names of Wales* and **J. J. Kneen**: *Place-names of the Isle of Man*. A combined work by **W. F. Nicolaisen, M. Gelling and M. Richards**, *The Names of Towns and Cities in Britain*, is a dictionary of the names of larger towns in England, Wales and Scotland and has a useful appendix on Greater London names. **A. Room**: *Dictionary of Place-names in the British Isles* includes also those of Ireland, as does **J. Field**: *Place-names of Great Britain and Ireland*. An account of early names as recorded by classical authors is given in **A. L. Rivet and Colin Smith**: *The Place-names of Roman Britain*.

Special topics are discussed in detail in **E. Ekwall**: *English River-names*, **J. Field**: *English Field-names: A Dictionary* and *A History of English Field-names* and **A. Room**: *The Street-names of England*. For a comprehensive bibliography, with critical comments, see **J. Spittal and J. Field**: *A Reader's Guide to the Place-names of the United Kingdom*, which contains information on all important books and articles on place-names and related topics published since 1920.

ORGANISATIONS

The Society for Name Studies in Britain and Ireland (formerly The Council for Name Studies) arranges an annual conference, in turn in Ireland, Scotland, Wales and England. Membership (open to all persons interested in place-names and personal names) includes a subscription to the annual publication, *Nomina*, containing conference papers, other relevant articles, items of news, and bibliographies. For details apply to Ms Jennifer Scherr, Queen's Building Library, University of Bristol, University Walk, Bristol BS8 1TH.

Members of the **English Place-Name Society** receive, each year, the Society's county volume and a copy of the *Journal*. They may also obtain some other EPNS publications at reduced prices. Nearly thirty of the ancient counties of England have been studied by the Society, surveys of five others are in course of publication, and three are in the early stages of preparation. A catalogue and membership details may be obtained from the Honorary Secretary, EPNS, School of English Studies, The University, Nottingham NG7 2RD.

Local place-name organisations have been formed, or are in process of formation, in various parts of Wales. Information about the **Clwyd Place-name Council** may be obtained from the Director, Dr Hywel Wyn Owen, Bryn Coed, Bron Haul, Llandegfan, Ynys Mon, Gwynedd LL59 5TL. Dr Owen may also be able to provide details of other place-name organisations in Wales.

Everyone interested in place-names will greatly benefit by joining **The British Association for Local History** and by taking part in activities the Association arranges in various parts of Britain. The twice yearly *Newsletter*, sent free to all members, publicises courses, exhibitions, conferences and new local history projects. The quarterly journal, *The Local Historian*, contains articles and book reviews of value to students of names and sometimes includes contributions specifically on these topics. For details of membership, apply to the Honorary Secretary, BALH, Shopwyke Manor Barn, Chichester, West Sussex PO20 6BG.

Index of place-names

The index lists every name explained, apart from field-names and street-names. Names are followed (as in the text) by an abbreviated county name, as given in the table of abbreviations. Rivers and mountains are usually noted.

65

INDEX

INDEX

70